BREWERY ADVENTURES IN THE WILD WEST

Jack Erickson

RedBrick Press

RESTON, VIRGINIA

To my father, Leo Erickson

BREWERY ADVENTURES IN THE WILD WEST

Copyright © 1991 by Jack Erickson

Published by:
RedBrick Press
Reston, VA 22090

ISBN 0-941397-04-1

Cover design: Barbara Flores Design, Berkeley, California

Erickson, Jack.
  Brewery adventures in the wild west : a directory of western
microbreweries and brewpubs / Jack Erickson. --
    p. cm.
  Includes bibliographical references and index.
  ISBN 0-941397-04-1
    1. Brewing industry--West (U.S.)--Directories. 2. Breweries--West
(U.S.)--Directories. 3. Brewing industry--West (U.S.)--Guide-books.
4. Breweries--West (U.S.)--Guide-books. 5. Brewing industry--
Canada, Western--Directories. 6. Breweries--Canada, Western--
Directories. 7. Brewing industry--Canada, Western--Guide-books. 8.
Breweries--Canada, Western--Guide-books. I. Title.

HD9397.U5   338.766342
                             QBI91-467

Library of Congress Catalog Card Number: 91-62216

First Edition

First Printing: September, 1991

Manufactured in the United States of America

10 9 8 7 6 5 4 3 2

TABLE OF CONTENTS

Acknowledgments   1

The Story Behind The Book   3

Introduction   9

State of the Industry   14

Northern California   31
Brewing by the Bay

Northwest   80
Munich on the Columbia

Southwest   139
Microbreweries Blooming in the Desert

Rocky Mountains   167
Microbrewing on the Range

Pacific Rim   193
Microbrewing in the Tropics and the Arctic

Index   202

Books by Jack Erickson
Published by RedBrick Press

STAR SPANGLED BEER
A Guide to America's New Microbreweries and Brewpubs

GREAT COOKING WITH BEER

ACKNOWLEDGMENTS

Many people were helpful in getting this book into print. Mike Abraham of the Vienna Inn in Vienna, Virginia, was as supportive as he always has been with RedBrick Press's ventures; Greg Kitsock of Washington, D.C., was a diligent researcher and writer; Rolando Garces and Rachel Woods of Garces Communications in Reston, Virginia, were creative in design and production; and Pat George of Purcellville, Virginia, was a patient proofreader. Barbara Flores of Berkeley, California, designed the cover.

Dr. Rolf Olness of Sonoma, California, a boyhood friend from North Dakota, served as an entertaining host on numerous trips to the West Coast; Charlotte Boxer of Portland, Oregon, was a generous hostess; the Erma Boxer family -- Erma, Francine, Mary Ann, Betty Jo and Hank Stein of Spokane, Washington -- were supportive in their own ways; and my father, Leo Erickson, in Williston, North Dakota, Lee and Becky Erickson and Diane and Jim Brandt of Glasgow, Montana, were always there with encouragement and enthusiasm. Shirley Schulz of Herndon, Virginia, was a supportive companion on many parts of this adventure.

Information was collected from many sources including *American Brewer, New Brewer, All About Beer, World Beer*

Review, California Celebrator, Cascade Beer News, the Institue for Brewing Studies in Boulder, Colorado, and the Beer Institute in Washington, D.C.

A special note of appreciation goes to the North American microbrewers themselves who completed the surveys and answered numerous phone calls and requests during 15 months of research and writing.

Many microbrewers were generous hosts on my trips to the West Coast. I appreciate their friendship and encouragement while this book was incubating.

THE STORY BEHIND THE BOOK

Every book has a story behind it. This story is not restricted
to the words on the pages. It includes the events that led to getting
it into print -- the premise of the book, the method of obtaining
the information, the motivation to tell the story, and what the book
was meant to accomplish. Every book proceeds along its own
evolutionary course from idea, to concept, to the research, the
outline and the writing of the manuscript, to the published book.
This book is no different.

The story behind "Brewery Adventures in the Wild West"
began four years ago when I wrote "Star Spangled Beer: A Guide
to America's New Microbreweries and Brewpubs." Along the
way, I traveled more than 30,000 miles throughout North
America and met many of the first generation of microbrewers:
Fritz Maytag of San Francisco's Anchor Brewery, Paul Shipman
of Seattle's Independent Ale Brewery, Paul Hadfield of
Victoria's Spinnakers Brewpub, Bill Newman of Albany's
Newmans Brewery, Matthew Reich of Manhattan's New
Amsterdam, Jim Koch of the Boston Beer Company, Bert Grant
of the Yakima Brewing Company, and Bill Owens of Hayward,
California's Buffalo Bill's Brewpub.

After the book was published in 1987, I continued to travel to
keep abreast of the changes going on in the emerging

microbrewing industry and to meet the new brewers. What intrigued me was that the microbrewing movement that started as a "mom and pop" phenomenon in the 1970's was evolving during the 1980's into a mini-industry that was revolutionizing the way beer was brewed and the way people perceived beer.

Consumers were awakening to the fact that beer was not just a generic product manufactured by a few household name megabrewers. It was a product with great diversity and a romantic history and culture all its own. Microbrewing was reviving an interest in the history of brewing in both the United States and Canada and the role it once played in both nations' culture and economy. Craft brewing was finding consumers appreciative of the new products which also captured the attention of entrepreneurs, the media, venture capital firms, business schools, and the megabreweries themselves.

It was my belief then, and continues to be today, that the North American microbrewing movement is the laboratory for a worldwide brewing revolution that will see craft breweries starting up throughout Asia, Europe, Australia, New Zealand, Japan, and even the Soviet Union and China. If anyone doubts the potential of a worldwide microbrewing revolution, all they need to do is visit a few of the microbreweries listed in this book. They'll understand why craft breweries are the wave of the future.

The reasoning is simple: 1) beer is the world's most popular alcoholic beverage; 2) consumers are bored with the lack of taste in industrial-produced beers; 3) consumers are drinking less alcohol but still seeking quality; and, 4) brewing specialty beers can be a profitable enterprise for visionary entrepreneurs.

It is no longer a question of whether a microbrewing revolution is going to occur, but how big it is going to be. The issues today are how it will evolve, what the major breweries will do to respond to it, the microbreweries' response to increased competition, and what consumers will support in terms of choices in beer styles.

NOT A NUMBERS GAME

When I first started writing about microbreweries in 1985, there were only about 40 of them and most were on the West Coast. When "Star Spangled Beer" was published in 1987, it listed 100 microbreweries in North America. The numbers have continually grown: 120 in 1988; 180 in 1989; and 280 in 1990.

But microbrewing has always been more than just a numbers game; it's an industry evolving across North America. A Belgian-style ale that sells by the carload in Seattle might fail in Dallas; a contract-brewed amber lager that wins national awards might sell on the East Coast but face resistance in the Northwest. An English-style pub might win over consumers in Minneapolis but draw little support in Atlanta.

The success of a microbrewery can be judged by how well its owners have anticipated the local market's taste preference in beer and how well they are able to brew that product. The obverse is also true: two award-winning ale-brewing microbreweries in Albany, New York, and Little Rock, Arkansas, failed in the 1980s because the local market for ales was not there despite the quality of the products. Had those ales been brewed on the West Coast where ales have greater acceptance, Newman's Brewery and Arkansas Brewing might still be operating.

A "BREWING RENAISSANCE"

The era of the 1980s was a heady time for microbrewing. Everyone was predicting great things for the future -- brewpubs on every university campus and microbreweries in towns all over the country. A "brewing renaissance" was the term that people in the industry uttered with confidence. America finally was emerging with creativity from the shadow cast by that old demon Prohibition.

In 1989, I wrote "Great Cooking With Beer" after observing the ways consumers were waking up not only to specialty beers but to the foods that could be prepared or served with them. People were matching foods with specialty beers in the same manner they had been pairing wines with food for years. I worked with restaurants and hotels to design dinners where we would match 12-15 specialty beers with three or four-course dinners and I would talk about beer tasting and cuisine. The response was overwhelmingly enthusiastic; consumers loved the dinners and restaurants were eager to promote specialty beers.

THE 1990'S -- THE DECADE OF BEER

The decade of the 1990s has seen no decline in interest in microbreweries and specialty beers. A trade publication predicts this will be the "Decade of Beer." Television's Discovery channel broadcast with good reviews Michael Jackson's series, "The Beer Hunter," featuring famous breweries. Publications that cover the microbrewing industry --*All About Beer, American Brewer, New Brewer, World Beer Review, California Celebrator,* and *Cascade Beer News* -- are filled with stories of microbrewery openings, new imports, beer festivals, the revival of old beer styles, restaurants hosting beer dinners, and brewery tours of Europe. The "Decade of Beer" is already with us.

In time, the microbrewing industry will be covered by the media much the way the wine and distilling industries are featured. For some reason, decision makers in the major newspapers, magazines, and electronic media consider beer a "second class" industry, possibly because of the blue-collar connotations that beer has had for decades.

Craft breweries have done much during the last ten years to change the way consumers regard beer. The media has been less responsive to this change.

WHY A WEST COAST MICROBREWERY GUIDE?

As a journalist, I've had this quaint idea to write a continuing history of the microbrewing revolution by periodically updating "Star Spangled Beer." Nevertheless, before I started to write the first revision, I decided to do a West Coast guide because the movement was born and enjoying its most creative expansion there. A travel guide to the 140 microbreweries and brewpubs from Vancouver to Sante Fe would reveal the depth and breadth of microbrewing in North America and the potential for a worldwide microbrewing revolution.

In my travels I have met hundreds of tourists, food connoisseurs, reporters, beer "groupies," and prospective microbrewers who wanted to know why it was happening. I was bombarded with questions: Where were other microbreweries? What kinds of beers did they brew? What were the best beers? How much money does it take to build a brewery?

Everyone hungered for more information -- not just about the location of the breweries and the beers they brewed, but also about why it was happening and what it meant for the future. Were the big breweries worried? (I doubt it.) Were more microbreweries going to open? (Definitely!) Is it easy to start one? (Nope.) How much money does it cost to open a microbrewery? (It depends.)

"Brewery Adventures in the Wild West" is designed for the adventurous traveler who wants to visit West Coast microbreweries and for armchair travelers who have never been to one. But the book is more than a travel guide -- it's also an overview of the craft brewing industry, a directory of 140 microbreweries and brewpubs, with a dash of history, folklore, and fun thrown in.

To write this book I traveled throughout the Western states and provinces and drove thousands of miles to visit microbreweries, meet the brewers, taste the beers, and get "the story behind the story." For the last year I sent surveys and wrote and called the microbreweries to get information on the state of the industry in the early 1990s.

Of the 140 microbreweries featured in the book, I have been to approximately 100. I hope it's not long before I get to those I missed this time around. So read on, have your "Brewery Adventure," and find out about this curious and wonderful phenomenon. It's an intriguing story that you're going to be hearing more about in the future.

INTRODUCTION

2 COUNTRIES

13 STATES -- 2 PROVINCES

61 BREWPUBS -- 82 MICROBREWERIES

532 BEERS!

This book has one objective -- to help the tourist, business traveler, beer lover, or adventurer plan a tour of 140 craft breweries in the West. Along the way you'll learn about the West Coast microbrewing revolution and, I hope, develop an appreciation for hand-crafted, specialty beers.

For decades it has been possible to tour great European cities and visit famous breweries featured in guidebooks and travel magazines. Centuries-old breweries in Great Britain, Belgium, Denmark, and Germany are part of European culture and history. They represent what the popular culture expects of a brewery -- classic red brick buildings, copper brew kettles boiling away, tasting rooms, beer gardens, and damp cellars housing wooden barrels. Artisans toiled a lifetime in these classic breweries balancing the science of brewing with traditional craftsmanship to produce beers famous around the world. European communities boast of their breweries and their traditions. And every year tourists sample beers and gain an appreciation for the craft of brewing and the prominence that breweries enjoy in the local culture. Brewing in Europe is not just a manufacturing process -- it is a revered tradition linked to the earliest days of civilization.

AT LAST - - BREWERIES WORTH VISITING

Until a few years ago, there was little comparable in the United States or Canada to the classic European breweries. With a couple exceptions, such as Anheuser-Busch's St. Louis home brewery, there were few North American breweries that looked like anything more than an industrial plant. There was little to look forward to in touring these brewing factories other than the obligatory stop in the tasting room. And the beers were no more distinctive than those found at any liquor store, convenience shop or restaurant. The beer was common and so were the breweries.

After Prohibition, brewing in North America became a manufacturing enterprise that produced similar beers that were hawked principally through loud and sexist TV advertising. The one compliment made about major breweries was that they were consistent -- they produced the same pale pilsener beer. Not exactly the kind of industry to arouse consumers' passions.

But this situation began to change in the late 1970s when microbreweries appeared in California, Oregon, Washington, and British Columbia. Although all their beers may not have been premium products, microbreweries offered a choice in beer styles and a qualitative difference with fresh and sometimes unfiltered, unpasteurized beer. Not the kind of products that would interest national breweries.

Microbreweries also generated creativity, excitement -- and even a little eccentricity: spicy ales, hearty amber lagers, creamy stouts, and delicious Christmas ales. Again, these were products that major breweries would have a difficult time marketing without a risk. The major breweries in North America, after all, have been quite successful in knowing what the majority of consumers want in beer styles and they supply that demand quite profitably.

A NEW BREWING TRADITION EMERGES IN THE WEST

That post-Prohibition cultural void is now, thankfully, being filled by the blossoming of craft breweries -- principally throughout Western North America. In British Columbia mountain resorts, seaside Oregon brewpubs, dusty Montana cowboy towns, and trendy California restaurants, microbreweries are awakening new respect for the world's oldest and most popular fermented beverage.

Since the mid-1980s, North American microbreweries have become a vibrant and dynamic industry with their own excitement and vision. Suppliers cater to customers they might have turned away a few years ago; brewing consultants fly from coast-to-coast to meet prospective clients; equipment manufacturers compete to sign up budding brewing ventures as soon as the ink on their business plan is dry; trade journals advertise feverishly for qualified brewers; and new microbreweries are opening weekly from Alaska and the Maritimes to Maine, Florida, and California.

There is a new appreciation for brewing. The title of brewer earns respect. The honor of having a brewery is something that communities fight for. Craft breweries are destination points for tourists looking for a new experience. The revival of craft brewing has made people eager to visit breweries and watch a brewer at work -- checking fermentation tanks, adding hops, pitching yeast, flowing the aromatic mixture to storage vessels, and finally, sampling his creation.

A tour of a brewery, of course, ends in a hospitality room for a glass of fresh beer that hours before was resting in storage tanks. Not a bad way to spend a couple of hours.

TEN "BREWERY ADVENTURE" CITIES

So you want to see what all the excitement is about?

Maybe you live in California, are a student in Seattle, have a business trip to Phoenix, or are going on a family vacation to British Columbia. This book will help you plan a brewery adventure in the West. It's easy to organize, takes little to plan, and has few limitations other than the time you want to invest.

And what in the world is a brewery adventure?

The requirements are simple: any city (or area) in the Western states and provinces where it is possible to visit four microbreweries -- including two brewpubs -- in one day. The tour could include lunch in one brewpub, a tour of two microbreweries during the rest of the day, and possibly dinner and a couple of beers in the second brewpub that evening. The time in between could be used for shopping, taking the kids to the zoo, visiting a museum, or going to a baseball game.

Visiting microbreweries qualifies as a family activity since virtually all of them make children as welcome as their parents. Restaurants that serve alcohol certainly don't discriminate against families; brewpubs are no different since they are restaurants as much as they are small breweries.

This book is organized so that travelers can tour through the five geographic regions in the West where it is possible to visit four microbreweries or brewpubs in one day. (San Francisco, Seattle, and Portland would require two or three days.) Armed with this book and a map, readers can plan a brewery adventure and a few other activities along the way.

Ten Western cities currently have enough microbreweries to qualify as "brewery adventure" cities:

Denver/Boulder

Los Angeles

Phoenix

Portland

Oakland/Berkeley

San Diego

San Francisco

Seattle

Vancouver

Victoria

PLANNING YOUR BREWPUB ADVENTURES

Tuck this book under your arm or slip it into your briefcase to look through while planning your trip. Then get a map and start charting a course on your North American Brewery Adventure. You might want to order a brewpub map ($3) from the American Brewer Magazine (3082 B. Street, Haywood, CA 98899).

You'll find a part of Americana or Canadiana that your grandparents knew when the countries were younger (and so were they!) and breweries were an exciting part of the nations' culture. After all, breweries are as American (and Canadian) as baseball, apple pie, Chevrolet, and, well, having a beer!

Have a good time, enjoy the beers, and say hello to the brewers for me. When you get back home, let me know about your brewery adventures and what you liked.

Visit a microbrewery today -- and become a part of the great North American microbrewing revolution!

THE STATE OF THE INDUSTRY: MICROBREWING IN THE 1990'S

HOW IT ALL BEGAN ...

Fritz Maytag had no idea he was starting a revolution when he first walked into San Francisco's dilapidated Anchor Brewing in 1965. After Maytag heard that the city's last brewery was to close, he offered to rescue the failing brewery and, if all things went well, bring brewing back to San Francisco, which had been home to more than 100 breweries at the turn of the century.

Maytag spent years learning every aspect of commercial brewing: distributing, marketing, accounting -- and brewing. His goal was to revive steam beer, a hybrid style brewed by San Francisco's breweries since the 1850s Gold Rush days.

Maytag also began brewing a variety of beer styles that had died out after Prohibition -- porter, ale, stout and barley wine. In 1975, Maytag brewed a special Christmas beer that was so popular that Anchor brewed it through the rest of the year and named it Liberty Ale in commemoration of America's 1976 Bicentennial.

One of Maytag's contributions to microbrewing was his revival of classic beer styles that once enjoyed popularity throughout the country. And although these beer styles may never reach wide acceptance through mass marketing, they represent the centuries-old craftsmanship in brewing. This revival of classic beer styles is part of the brewing renaissance that has received so much attention and appreciation from consumers for a nearly-lost art rediscovered. In 1988, Maytag was awarded the Institute for Brewing Studies' Achievment Award for his contributions to brewing.

The array of Anchor's products include steam beer, porter, ale, wheat, barleywine, and Christmas ale.

NEW ALBION & SIERRA NEVADA

An even more quixotic microbrewing venture began during the summer of 1977 in the heart of California's wine country. Thirty one-year-old Jack McAuliffe, an ex-sailor who had fallen in love with English-style ales in Scotland, started brewing in a warehouse leased from a fruit company on the outskirts of Sonoma. McAuliffe called his brewery New Albion, which was the name Sir Francis Drake gave California when he sailed into San Francisco Bay in the 16th century. (New Albion's label showed Drake's Golden Hind sailing through the Golden Gate.)

After a few setbacks -- including the loss of his starter yeast strain -- McAuliffe began selling New Albion Pale Ale in the fall of 1977 in Sonoma County. "We intend to make Sonoma Valley as famous for ale, porter, and stout as it is for the wines, cheeses, and French bread," McAuliffe boasted.

But McAuliffe's venture lacked capital and he had trouble producing a consistent quality. He sold New Albion Pale Ale, Porter, and Stout, but not enough to stay alive as a business. In 1982, he was forced to close even though the Sonoma County zoning board had approved plans for New Albion's new 5,000 sq. ft. brewery on east Napa Street.

In 1978, two more young California homebrewers, Paul Camusi and Ken Grossman, started the Sierra Nevada Brewery in Chico, home of Chico State College. Camusi and Grossman were fortunate enough to have the backing of Maytag, who sold them used brewing equipment to get started. With a meager $110,000, they constructed their small brewery in 1979 and immediately began winning awards for their distinctive ales.

Sierra Nevada followed the model of Anchor by developing an impressive portfolio of beer styles that seemed exotic when they first appeared; today those same beers are benchmarks which other microbreweries use to gauge their own products

Sierra Nevada's award winning beers brewed in Chico include their pale ale, stout, porter, bigfoot, and Celebration Ale.

MICROBREWING COMES TO BRITISH COLUMBIA

The Anchor, New Albion, and Sierra Nevada microbrewing ventures captured the imaginations of the media and numerous stories appeared in West Coast publications about these odd and puzzling happenings. In British Columbia, three adventurous Canadians who had read about California's first microbreweries came up with the idea to brew beer and sell it through a restaurant. Dave Patrick, Don Wilson, and John Mitchell began building a small brewery north of Vancouver in scenic Horseshoe Bay and contacted the Troller Pub 100 yards away.

The Canadian trio's first obstacle was convincing the B.C. Liquor Control and Licensing Branch that they were a serious business venture and not just eccentric hobbyists. Mitchell hired David Bruce-Thomas, who worked as a bartender at Troller, to become their brewer. In June 1982, the Horseshoe Bay Brewery/Troller Pub became North America's first "brewpub" restaurant. Horseshoe Bay/Troller's first beers were English-style ales: Bay Ale, Royal Ale, and Pale Ale. (John Mitchell later moved on to help start Spinnakers Brewpub on Victoria's Inner Harbor).

The interest in microbrewing in Canada was not limited to Horseshoe Bay's start-up. At the same time, two other British Columbia entrepreneurs, Mitchell Tayler and Bill Harvey, were raising money to start a microbrewery in Vancouver. They hired veteran brewer Rainer Kallahne and in June 1984, opened Granville Island Brewing. Their first two beers were Island Lager and Island Bock.

BREWPUBS START IN WASHINGTON & CALIFORNIA

South of the 39th parallel, the brewery in a restaurant concept got its start in a fitting setting. In Washington's sunny Yakima Valley famous for growing apples, pears, and peaches (as well as world-famous hops), Yakima Brewing and Malting opened its doors in 1982 in an old opera house. Yakima Brewery's founder was Bert Grant, who wanted to imitate the neighborhood atmosphere of British pubs complete with "pub grub," darts, and freshly-brewed ales.

As a brewing chemist with nearly four decades of international experience, Grant was the first veteran brewer to enter the new microbrewing mini-industry. Grant's ales, stouts, and ciders won widespread approval of both consumers and beer judges from their earliest days. His Russian Imperial Stout revived a style that dated from 19th century English breweries that produced special batches for Russia's Romanov Tsars.

A year later, brewpubs arrived in California where microbrewing not only started but has shown its most dynamic growth. The state's first brewpub opened in tiny Hopland in Mendocino County on August 14, 1983. Hopland's brewers were Don Barkley and Michael Lovett, who had brewed at New Albion under McAuliffe.

A month later, a former award-winning photographer, Bill Owens, opened the state's second brewpub -- Buffalo Bill's -- in Hayward. From the moment he opened his funky brewpub, Owens became a colorful proponent for the microbrewing movement. Bill has rarely been shy about sharing a clever quip about microbrewing for journalists hungry for local color.

THE FIRST GENERATION OF WEST COAST MICROBREWERS

In hindsight, it's not difficult to speculate why microbrewing started in California. Sociologists and cultural gurus who study lifestyles consider California the nation's hothouse where trends first become reality. Many of these trends are unorthodox, but a few have staying power and survive the marketplace to change peoples' attitudes about what they eat, drink, watch on TV, or how they spend their leisure time.

Microbrewing's pioneers changed peoples' thinking about the beer they drank. They offered something other than another fizzy pale pilsener that tasted just like any other beer. An example is Anchor's Christmas Ale, that not only has become a classic in its own right, but also established a tradition for other West Coast microbreweries.

Early microbreweries revived the art of brewing seasonal beers. Most popular have been the annual Christmas beers which are usually darker, spicier ales -- often brewed with spices and abundant aromatic hops.

Sierra Nevada's Celebration Ale, Redhook's Winterhook, Boulder's Christmas Stout, Hale's Celebration Ale, Thomas Kemper's Winterbrau, Hart's Snow Cap Stout, Widmer's Fest, Kessler's Holiday, and Yakima's Russian Imperial Stout are just a few holiday beers that have become annual treats for loyal customers. Even Coors, the nation's third largest brewery, brews Winterfest as its seasonal offering. Coors' venture into seasonal beers is testimony to the fact that traditions begun by microbreweries can be adopted successfully by national breweries.

THE SHAKE OUT BEGINS

But all was not rosy for the microbrewing pioneers. Just because a microbrewery is one of the first to open does not mean it has the capital, business experience, product, distribution, or resources to survive. Brewing is a high-risk, capital-intensive industry for newcomers and seasoned companies alike. Brewing has always been a volatile commercial undertaking.

New Albion was not the only early West Coast microbrewery to fail. The Cartwright Brewery in Portland, DeBakker Brewery in Marin County, and River City in Sacramento all started and closed in the early 1980s. But that didn't stop homebrewers as well as experienced businessmen with little brewing background from taking the leap to become microbrewers.

In Portland, the Widmer family started a brewery specializing in German-style Alt beers; in Seattle, Paul Shipman helped start Independent Ale in the Ballard industrial area; in Colville, Washington, Mike Hale started Hales Ales; in Kalama, Washington, Tom and Beth Baune started Hart Brewery in the shadow of Mt. St. Helens, and a group of homebrewing professors from the University of Colorado started Boulder Brewing in Boulder. Today, these Western microbreweries are brewing some of the finest beers produced in North America.

Pioneers from the early 1980's who have survived to become well-respected members of the Western microbrewing fraternity: Widmer (Portland), Thomas Kemper (Poulsbo), Redhook (Seattle), Hales (Colville and Kirkland), Boulder (Boulder), Buffalo Bill's (Hayward), Pyramid (Kalama), Mendocino (Hopland), and Grants (Yakima).

By the mid-1980s, a new generation of North American entrepreneurs replaced the pioneers who came mostly from a homebrewing background. This new generation had business experience and knew how to attract venture capital. They could study a P & L sheet as well as analyze a hop's bittering units.

This second generation of businessmen are representative of the individuals now entering microbrewing and see it as a serious business venture. They acknowledge the risks but also anticipate the financial benefits from understanding the intricacies of marketing, accounting, finance and distribution. After all, it takes more than brewing beer to be a successful brewer.

THE GREAT AMERICAN BEER FESTIVAL

As the microbrewing movement was going through its growing pains, a forum for displaying its products -- a national beer festival -- came from a trade assocation originally organized for homebrewers. In 1982, the American Homebrewers Association (AHA) held the first Great American Beer Festival (GABF) in Denver. The first festival was modestly successful and plans were made to hold it annually.

Today, the GABF serves as the annual gathering for microbrewers from all over the United States to "show their stuff" at two nights of beer tasting. AHA sponsors organized a Best Beer in America contest with attendees voting for their favorite beers. For the early years of the GABF, the Best Beers in America contest was considered as "gentlemanly competition" with little fanfare or notoriety.

But in 1985, the Best Beer in America contest was criticized by small brewers when Samuel Adams Boston Lager won after an aggressive promotion by brewery employees at the GABF. The protest continued when Samuel Adams won the next two years, even though other brewers started campaigning for votes. Amidst charges of ballot stuffing and vote buying, AHA officials changed the rules for the contest. A professional beer judging panel was organized to award medals in distinct beer styles.

The Great American Beer Festival in Denver hosted by the American Homebrewers Association is one of the major beer festivals in North America. Brewers annually showcase their beers at the GABF for both colleagues and consumers. The consumer preference poll has been replaced by professional judges who award medals in 31 brewing styles. Western microbreweries have always done well at the GABF.

Finally, in 1990, the GABF eliminated the consumer preference voting as the Best Beer in America award was called and expanded the professional judging panel. Judges sampled and awarded medals in 31 beer styles in 10 ale categories (amber, barley wine, brown, pale, etc.); 14 lager categories (amber/vienna, American lager, bock, doppelbock, European pilsener, etc.) ; and 7 hybrid categories (alt, American wheat, fruit, spice, weizen, etc.).

West Coast microbreweries have always done well in both the Best Beer in America competition and in the judging panels. At the 1990 GABF, 46 of the 80 beers that received medals were brewed by West Coast microbreweries. Of the 25 medals awarded for ales, all but 1 were awarded to West Coast microbreweries. All the medals in the Amber Ale, Barley Wine, Blond/Golden Ale, Brown Ale, Pale Ale, Strong Ale, and Fruit styles were awarded to West Coast microbreweries. Further, in 17 of the 31 categories, the Gold Medal winner was the product of a West Coast microbrewery.

The GABF was a bellwether of what was to come. Once the only beer festival in American, the GABF is now one of several annual West Coast beer festivals. San Francisco's KQED TV hosts a beer and food festival every July as do the Northwest microbrewers at the Oregon Beer Festival in Portland.

Even though the Oregon Beer Festival has been held only since 1988, it is already the largest beer festival in North America. In 1990, an estimated 25,000 people attended the three-day affair the last weekend in July. Microbreweries from as far away as Massachusetts, Minnesota, and Colorado were represented among the 40 breweries attending. "In the Northwest, we have the most sophisticated beer consumer in the country," said Jim McConnaughey who publishes the *Cascade Beer News* bi-monthly newsletter in Portland. "We're looking at a new Munich here in terms of a beer culture in America."

Throughout the West Coast, beer festivals are held at state and county fairs, restaurant shows, and various sponsored events. Spokane and San Diego public TV stations have sponsored beer events, as has the Fogg n' Sudds restaurant chain in British Columbia.

THE MICROBREWING "LABORATORY"

Even though microbreweries are well-established around North America, the West Coast remains the heart of the movement -- and probably always will be. A tolerant attitude toward new trends makes ventures like boutique breweries more likely to find a receptive market from consumers looking for something different.

In many ways, the last 15 years has proven that the West is the laboratory for North American craft brewing. A variety of small brewing enterprises has started up there and most are still operating. Investors and potential microbrewers from other parts of North America usually include a trip West to study the early microbreweries and to learn what they did to remain in business.

An indication of the significance of the West Coast microbreweries is that most of the microbrewing "firsts" occurred in the West. They include:

- First microbrewery: Anchor - 1965
- First "start-up" microbrewery: New Albion - 1976
- First Canadian microbrewery: Granville Island (British Columbia) - 1986
- First Canadian brewpub: Horseshoe Bay (British Columbia) - 1982
- First American brewpub: Yakima - 1982
- First microbrewery that started as a brewpub: Yakima - 1982
- First chain of brewpubs: McMenamin's first brewpub - Hillsdale Brewery & Public House - 1985. (McMenamin's chain now includes 11 Portland and Northern Oregon brewpubs)
- First microbrewery to offer contract brewing services: Montana Beverage (Kessler Brewing) - 1987
- First microbrewery to also contract brew at an established brewery: Boulder - 1988

The West continues to lead in most areas of microbrewing except one -- contract brewing (hiring brewing services from a conventional brewery and developing a market before building a brewery). Although a few Western micros began as contract operations (Pete's Brewing, Sun Valley), contract brewing remains a Midwestern and Eastern approach to microbrewing. Purists have little regard for contract brewers and consider them as marketing operations. Nevertheless, contract brewing represents a creative way to start a microbrewing venture.

CATEGORIES OF MICROBREWERIES

The microbrewing industry has had relatively loose definitions. For years the definition offered by the American

Homebrewers Association was limited to a production figure --
a brewery whose production was less than 10,000 barrels/year.
That number was later increased to 15,000 barrels/year.

I prefer a more descriptive qualifier since a definition restricted
to production implies that volume makes a microbrewery
significant. I choose to define a microbrewery as one with limited
production (less than 50,000 barrels/year) and offering a selection
of specialty beers: amber lagers, ales, porters, stouts, wheat, and
seasonal beers that are not part of the inventory of major brewers.
Major brewers generally confine themselves to variations on the
pilsener theme (drys and lites included) with only a rare seasonal
or specialty beer (Coors Winterfest).

Since the term microbrewery is used without much
explanation, it does not give any hint of what type of
microbreweries exist. They range from one or two-man
operations like the Nevada City Brewing, Roslyn Brewing, and
Etna Brewing in rural communities, to the elegant Anchor, Sierra
Nevada, and Redhook Breweries.

Tremendous diversity exists depending on the size of
operation, sophistication of equipment, style of beer, distribution
network, and level of marketing. In general, there are six types
of microbreweries and brewpubs:

1) Regional Brewery: Anchor, Redhook, Sierra Nevada
   (An operation that exceeds more than 25,000 barrels/year)
2) Microbrewery: Snake River, Hales Ales
   (Production of 5,000 barrels/year or less)
3) Mini-microbrewery: Pike Place
   (Limited distribution; less than 1,000 barrels/year)
4) Microbrewery/brewpub: Mendocino, Yakima
   (A brewpub that also sells off-premise; production varies)
5) Brewpub: Rogue River, Seabright
   (A brewpub with no off- premises sales)

6) Restaurant/brewpub: Truckee, Cave Junction
(A restaurant that added a brewery to its operation)

WEST COAST MICROBREWING SURVEY

A survey of 143 West Coast microbreweries indicates that California leads with 64 (18 micros and 46 brewpubs) followed by Oregon with 21 (6 micros and 15 brewpubs) and Washington with 14 (9 micros and 5 brewpubs). California is home to nearly half of the 143 West Coast microbreweries.

British Columbia has 11 microbreweries (7 micros and 4 brewpubs) but nationwide is third behind Ontario which has 35 microbreweries (10 micros and 25 brewpubs) and Quebec with 13 (7 micros and 6 brewpubs).

Together California (64) and Ontario (35) have more than 1/3 of North America's 280 microbreweries.

UNITED STATES

	Microbreweries	Brewpubs
Alaska	1	
Arizona	2	5
California	18	46 (5)*
Colorado	3	7 (1)*
Hawaii	2	
Idaho	1	
Montana	3	(1)*
Nevada	1	
New Mexico	1	1
Oregon	6	15 (2)*
Utah	1	1 (1)*
Washington	9	5 (3)*
Wyoming	1	
TOTAL	49	80

Total Microbreweries/Brewpubs — 129

CANADA

	Microbreweries	Brewpubs
Alberta	2	1
British Columbia	7	4 (1)*
TOTAL	9	5

Total Microbreweries/Brewpubs — 14

WEST COAST TOTALS
2 Canadian Provinces, 13 United States

	Microbreweries	Brewpubs
TOTAL	58	85

Total Microbreweries/Brewpubs — 143

(#) Information complied by the Institute for Brewing Studies and other sources.

* Indicates brewpub also sells off premise

WEST COAST BEER PUBLICATIONS THRIVING

Microbrewing has become such a dynamic industry that it has spawned a spirited trade press of newspapers, magazines, and newsletters. Not surprisingly, most are published in the West.

Largest of the publication is the bi-monthly magazine *All About Beer,* published in Oceanside, California, by Mike and Bunny Bosak. The Bosaks purchased the magazine from a Los Angeles publishing company that was more involved in automotive, martial arts, and firearms fields. In the two years since the Bosaks acquired *All About Beer,* they have improved the graphics and editorial coverage. They now report on international beer developments with regular coverage of microbreweries and brewpubs. (Bosak Publishing Co. 4764 Galicia Way, Oceanside, CA 92056; $20 for 6 issues)

An upstart publication is *American Brewer* magazine, published by Bill Owens of Buffalo Bill's Brewpub in Hayward. Owens purchased the name and mailing list from Portland beer writer Fred Eckhardt in 1988 and since then has added a special touch that makes each issue interesting and fun to read. *American Brewer's* coverage is oriented to profiles of leaders in microbrewing and articles on legal, technical, and business aspects of microbrewing. The latest openings and closings are featured as well as off-beat stories from the around the world about beer.

An entertaining column at the back of the book is "Billspeak" written by Owens who offers his trenchant views on attracting investors, beer publications, the media, and anything else he thinks can contribute to the microbrewing debate. (Box 510, Hayward, CA 94541, 415-538-9500; sample issue $3)

The American Homebrewers Association in Boulder, Colorado has been a prominent leader in the craft brewing movement. In 1987, the AHA organized the Institute for Brewing

Studies which compiles data from microbreweries and publishes the bi-monthly *New Brewer* , a trade magazine with ties to the suppliers, manufacturers, and consultants in the industry. AHA also publishes *Zymurgy* for the homebrewing market. (Box 287, Boulder, CO; $55 *New Brewer* subscription; $18 for *Zymurgy.)*

California Celebrator, started in 1988 by Bert and Julie Nickles, has quickly established itself as the premier West Coast sheet covering microbreweries. Available at liquor stores, restaurants, book stores, microbreweries, and gourmet food outlets, the *Celebrator* has become the most entertaining way to follow the microbrewing movement in California. (P.O. Box 375, Hayward, CA 94543; $14.95 annual subscription of 6 issues)

In Portland, Jim McConnaughey and Clyde Fulkerson publish their *Cascade Beer News* newsletter in magazine format covering Oregon, Washington, and British Columbia. CBN also covers the restaurant, taverns, and special events where beer is a main player. Look for great things from this paper.

Two smaller publication in Seattle cover the active Northwest brewing scene: the *Northwest Beer Journal* is an advertorial writing about the people who advertise; the *Pint Post,* published by the Microbrewing Appreciation Society (MAS) features interviews with microbrewing personalities and articles on Northwest brewing events.

MICROBREWERY TOURS

It was bound to happen -- microbrewery touring companies. In Seattle and San Francisco, private companies have started up to offer tours to local microbreweries and brewpubs.

The Towerbridge Group started tours in the Fall of 1989 to Seattle's six microbreweries and brewpubs. Half-day tours include beer tastings, transportation, souvenirs and a guide. Founder Brian O'Sullivan says the service is for international visitors, conventioneers, beer lovers and curious travelers who want to see what all the excitement is about with Seattle's microbreweries.

In San Francisco, Brewpub Tours offers tours to the two dozen microbreweries in the Bay Area. (415-553-ALES).

NORTHERN CALIFORNIA

BREWING BY THE BAY

Anyone who has been to San Francisco understands how a city could affect one's life. San Francisco is Paradise. Mystery. Excitement. The cable cars, hills, and winding streets of the City by the Bay are so seductive that visitors have forsaken jobs, careers, and families to move there and become a part of it.

It's no surprise that movies seeking to entice viewers with an air of adventure or romance frequently use San Francisco as a setting. Remember the breathtaking car chase scenes in Steve McQueen's "Bullitt," the adventures of Clint Eastwood's Dirty Harry, the backdrop of the Golden Gate Bridge in Alfred Hitchcock's "Vertigo," and Humphrey Bogart wandering through darkened streets in "The Maltese Falcon."

Advertisers call upon the picturesque San Francisco to deliver commercial messages: life is better when products have a connection to the panorama of the Golden Gate Bridge, the eerie night fog creeping over the city, the cold waters lapping against San Quentin's rocks, quaint cable cars clanging up Nob Hill, and teeming Chinatown.

Movies and popular culture have made San Francisco into more than a city -- it's a lifestyle of tolerance and creativity. However one's life is going, there is always the fantasy of escaping to San Francisco and starting over with no questions asked. Dreams are made -- and sometimes broken -- in the City by the Bay. But San Francisco's charm is not limited to the city; all of Northern California represents a special place in the imagination of anyone who has visited the area.

Northern California also has one of the country's most dynamic economies. The nation's computer industry started in Silicon Valley. The Sonoma and Napa Valleys are world famous for their wines. Area restaurants are known for their innovative cuisine. The ports of San Francisco and Oakland are crammed with goods from the Far East, and crowded San Francisco International Airport is a jumping-off point for Hong Kong, Singapore, Tokyo, Seoul, Auckland, Sydney, Taipei and Honolulu. Wrap these features together and they make Northern California one of the most exciting places in the world. Everything that makes life worthwhile -- beauty, nature, commerce, culture, and diversity -- are found in Northern California. It's little wonder that the area also represents the soul of the North American craft brewing industry.

BIRTHPLACE OF MICROBREWING

Northern California is a special place -- it was the birthplace of the North American microbrewing movement. The first two steps to revive craft brewing began 10 years apart and from both sides of the Golden Gate Bridge. The first, in San Francisco, exceeded by far the expectations of its visionary founder; the second, in Sonoma, floundered after an accumulation of problems that afflict most small business ventures -- insufficient capital, limited distribution, inadequte staff, and no business plan to survive in a competitive marketplace.

In 1965, Stanford graduate student Fritz Maytag bought the aging San Francisco Anchor Brewery south of Market Street as it was about to close. Eleven years later in a dusty shed in sunny Sonoma 45 miles north of the Golden Gate Bridge, ex-Navy sailor Jack McAuliffe turned a homebrewing hobby into a commercial brewery when he opened the New Albion Brewery.

Fritz Maytag, President of San Francisco's Anchor Brewery. Maytag is considered the guiding light of the North American microbrewing movement. One of his major accomplishments has been reviving classic beer styles such as steam beer, Amerian ale, wheat beer, Christmas wassail, and barley wine.

From those diverse beginnings, the North American microbrewing revolution was born. In the 25 years since Maytag began turning around the Anchor Brewery and McAuliffe started New Albion, their deeds were like casting stones on a pond. Microbrewing ripples that began in Northern California spread throughout the West Coast, over the Rocky Mountains, into the Midwest, back to the East Coast and all throughout Canada. Today there are two dozen microbreweries in the Bay area, almost 70 across the state, 140 in the Western states and provinces, and nearly 300 in North America.

Northern California illustrates the unlimited potential for craft brewing to find a home in virtually any location regardless of geography, economics, population, or brewing tradition. It is possible to drive throughout Northern California and never be more than an hour from fresh, hand-crafted beer produced by a microbrewery or brewpub.

Stockton. Chico. Hopland. Boonville. Ft. Bragg. Calistoga. Santa Rosa. Napa. Mountain View. San Jose. Palo Alto. Walnut Creek. Eureka. Oakland. Berkeley. Modesto. Santa Cruz. Monterey. Hayward. Davis. Fremont. Progressive city, modern suburb, farming community, resort, dusty ranching town, and campus locale -- they're all a part of the Northern California craft brewery movement that started modestly and grew into something that shows what creativity, tradition, and commerce can bring to an industry that had become staid and unimaginative.

The California craft brewing movement has as much to do with the law as it does with culture. The state was one of the first to legalize homebrewing in 1978 (it had actually been illegal since Prohibition) and to allow brewpubs to sell retail in 1983. These initiations owe no small debt to the small wineries that started in Northern California in the 1960s and transformed the nation's wine industry with its "small is beautiful" revolution.

California, of course, has long been the hotbed of trends whether they be food, music, education, language, customs or alcohol. If small wineries could start a trend that saw "boutique" wineries open in diverse states such as Texas, Virginia, Arkansas and Ohio, couldn't a similar nationwide trend happen with "boutique" breweries?

CALIFORNIA BEERS -- AND FOODS

California was also the first state to acknowledge the creative uses of foods with specialty beers. San Francisco chefs and food writers began promoting food and beer combinations after seeing how the California brewpubs designed their foods to be served and cooked with specialty beers.

The consensus among the chefs, food writers, and brewers is that the spicier ethnic foods such as Chinese, Thai, Indian, and Mexican dishes are ideal with beer, as are Americanized foods like chili, pizza, and barbeque. The creative aspect has been in finding the many wine-oriented foods such as seafoods, pasta dishes, meats, and desserts that can be matched with ales, porters, stouts and amber lagers which have specialized flavors, aromas, and textures reminiscent of wines.

The selection of specialty beers on the menu is not restricted to brewpubs and taverns. Well-known California restaurants Chez Panisse, Zuni, and the Dakota Grille have added specialty beers to their menu to keep up with consumer interest. The Stanford Court Hotel on Nob Hill has its own beer list, as do numerous other restaurants such as Dewey's in the Fairmont Hotel.

A WEEK OF BREWPUB CRAWLS

There are so many microbreweries in Northern California that it would take about a week to visit them all. It's a challenge for the adventurous beer traveler to see them all; the only limitations are time and a willingness to drive several hundred miles to visit them. The rewards are the beautiful scenery, the geographic diversity, the vast expanses of the state, as well as the breweries and their fine beers.

A busy Day One would start with visiting brewpubs and microbreweries in San Francisco and across the Bay Bridge in

Oakland and Berkeley. Days Two would be spent reaching microbreweries south of the Bay in Santa Cruz, Palo Alto, Mountain View, San Jose, and Hayward with Day Three heading north to the many microbreweries in Marin, Napa, Sonoma, and Mendocino counties.

Days Four and Five would involve driving up and down the coast toward Carmel and Monterey to the south or northward to Ft. Bragg or Boonville. Then, Days Six and Seven mean traveling inland to Davis, Sacramento, Lake Tahoe, and Chico.

If you don't have the time for a full week of brewpub crawling, make up your own brewery tour. A little of this, a little of that, and in a few days you'll have caught the fever of Northern California breweries. It's infectious, so give in to the urge and indulge. You'll have a great time, see some beautiful country, have good weather, we hope, and see why craft brewing is such an exciting aspect of life in Northern California. The possibilities are endless, the fun is limitless, and the beer matchless.

HISTORICAL LANDMARKS

The conscientious beer traveler would not consider a trip without making a pilgrimage to several microbrewing landmarks. Here are a few "must sees" for the brewery adventurer.

At the top of the list is the tour of San Francisco's Anchor Brewery south of Market Street on Mariposa Avenue. It's a little off the beaten path, but worth the 10 minute drive from downtown to see those gorgeous copper brewing vessels and sip those marvelous beers in the hospitality room.

A little further off the beaten path is a visit to Buffalo Bill's Brewpub in sleepy Hayward. If you are lucky, Buffalo Bill Owens himself may be brewing and you'll have a chance to hear a few minutes of his rambling, but passionate treatise on microbrewing. One day in the not-to-distant future, Buffalo Bill's may be designated a landmark by the National Preservation

Society with a plaque commemorating its historic significance as a mecca for a generation of aspiring microbrewers who began visiting when "Chairman" Bill first opened in September 1983.

Sierra Nevada in Chico, California brews ales considered some of the most distinctive in the world. It's new brewery and brewpub is both elegant and classic. It's worth a trip to Chico to see why Sierra Nevada continues to inspire potential new microbrewers.

A brewery adventurer should also consider a drive 90 miles north on Highway 101 to the Mendocino Brewery in tiny Hopland. Logging was once king in Mendocino County, but *cannabis* now seems the crop of choice in the wooded valleys. The Mendocino Brewery deserves recognition as California's first brewpub, opening in August 14, 1983 in the old Hopvine Saloon which in earlier life was also a butcher shop.

Mendocino also was the second home of the New Albion Brewery after founder Jack McAuliffe closed his Sonoma microbrewery. New Albion's equipment now rests in a shed in the back of Mendocino collecting dust and legends about its offspring. One hopes that New Albion's equipment will be moved one day to a Microbrewers Hall of Fame or suitable location where its accomplishments to the American pioneering spirit -- and good beer -- will be recognized.

Once this far north, the brewery adventurer is only a couple hours away from Chico, home of the legendary Sierra Nevada Brewery. Sierra Nevada's ales are deservedly considered world class. The new brewery, however, must be seen to appreciate the high standards that Sierra Nevada maintains in all its ventures.

CALIFORNIA CELEBRATOR -- COVERING THE CALIFORNIA BEER SCENE

Along the way, brewery adventurers will want to pick up a copy of *California Celebrator*, a breezy, bi-monthly newspaper published in Hayward. The *Celebrator* covers the California craft brewing scene with reviews, features, and announcements of new microbrewing openings from Eureka to San Diego.

The husband-and-wife team of Bret and Julie Nickels started the *Celebrator* in February 1988, with a 12-page issue and circulation of 10,000. Bret and Julie were working for a British Columbia restaurant chain when they discovered the rapidly emerging California microbrewing scene and returned home to start reporting on it. Three years later, *California Celebrator's* circulation is 40,000 with 24 ad-filled pages of easy prose and fun features of "all the news that's fit to drink."

The *Celebrator* covers other beer and microbrewery related news. Recent features reported on the Northwest microbrewing scene, Christmas beers, Oktoberfest festivals, British pubs in California, and beer and food combinations. The *Celebrator's* pool of writers and its location in the center of the California brewing movement makes it an American journalistic cousin of *What's Brewing*, the British newspaper published by the Campaign to Preserve Real Ale (CAMRA).

Pick up a copy. Subscribe for a modest fee ($14.95) and follow California's microbrewing scene so you'll be up-to-date when you return. (Box 375, Hayward, CA 94543; 415-670- 0121.)

BEER FESTIVALS

A visit to California microbreweries is not complete without attending one of the many beer festivals that take place nearly every week somewhere in the state. From Eureka to San Diego, beer festivals and tastings are held at county fairs, community and ethnic celebrations, restaurants, brewpubs and food events.

San Francisco's public TV station KQED sponsors an annual beer and food festival every July with microbreweries prominently featured. The California Small Brewers Festival in October in Mountain View is another event that features the state's microbrewed beers. The California Festival of Beers is held in May in San Luis Obispo at The Graduate. Check local papers, the *California Celebrator* and *American Brewer*, or ask at any brewpub to find out about the latest festival.

Although it is not a "festival," Lyon's Brewery in Dublin (it's neither a brewery nor in Ireland), is the closest one can come to sampling nearly every California microbrewed beer (and others from the West) any day of the year. Publican Judy Ashworth has assembled 34 beers on tap and over 100 specialty beers in an American pub in Central California deserving of a visit from any brewery adventurer. Recommended for its hospitality as well as its beers. (Town & Country Shopping Center, 7294 San Ramon Road, Dublin, CA 94568; 415-829-9071)

A popular chain of bars in San Francisco named Jacks also features "365 Days of Beer Festivals" and claims 106 taps at three locations. The Jacks are at 1601 Fillmore (22 beers on tap), 3200 16th Street (51 beers on tap), and 1300 Church (33 beers on tap).

SAN FRANCISCO
BERKELEY/OAKLAND

ANCHOR BREWING
1705 Mariposa Street
San Francisco 94107   415-863-8350
President: Fritz Maytag
Brewer: Mark Carpenter

Founded in 1896, San Francisco's Anchor Brewery was one of the city's 27 that prospered before Prohibition producing steam beer, a California specialty that traced its origins to 1850s Gold Rush days. Before refrigeration, lager beer could not be chilled and would build up enormous carbonation pressure in California's hot weather. When beer was tapped for serving, geysers of "steam" would explode from the barrel.

But after Repeal and decades of mergers, consolidations, and closures, Anchor was San Francisco's last brewery in the mid-1960s when Stanford Asian studies graduate student Frederick Louis Maytag III became interested in the tiny brewery. Using resources from the family's Iowa washing machine fortune, "Fritz" purchased a share of Anchor in 1965 and eventually bought ownership in 1969. He immersed himself in all phases of brewing and business and in 10 years had created a modern brewery producing specialty beers that had all but disappeared from America: porter, wheat beer, American ale, barleywine, Christmas beer, and the flagship steam beer which Anchor has trademarked in the U.S.

Today, Anchor is a Potrero Hill landmark and mecca for beer lovers, tourists, history buffs, and aspiring microbrewers. Tours end in the attractive taproom where visitors sip Anchor's fresh beers amidst brewing memorabilia.

Anchor Steam - *amber-colored classic fermented in shallow, open vessels; krausened to produce extra carbonation*
Anchor Porter - *almost black; abundant hops produce rich, mellow flavor*
Anchor Wheat - *brewed with 65% malted wheat; light, creamy head*
Liberty Ale - *aromatic, mildly sweet*
Anchor Christmas Ale - *first brewed in 1975; each annual recipe changes; recent offerings have been English-style wassails brewed with aromatic spices and numerous hop varieties*
Old Foghorn Barleywine - *aged for nine months, it reaches 8% alcohol by volume; a rich, sipping beer*

1989: 58,000 barrels
1990: 68,000 barrels

BISON BREWERY
2598 Telegraph Avenue
Berkeley 94704   415-841-7734
President: Eric Freitag
Brewer: Scott DeOca

Bison Brewpub was Bill Owens' third brewpub in Northern California when it opened in 1988 on a busy corner near the Berkeley campus. Bison is a typical Berkeley establishment and resembles a coffee house or espresso bar.

Bison's clientele is UC students -- a culturally mixed and free-spirited crowd. Accordingly, Bison has been on the leading edge of experimental brewing with spices and seasonal herbs such as honey and basil beer, cardamon ale, chocolate ale as well as ordinary stout, bitter, and red ale. Brewer Scott DeOca rotates brewing recipes with two beers on tap at all times.

Live music is featured on weekends and Berkeley artists' works are displayed on the walls. California microbrewered beers are on tap.

Brewpub menu: "earthy" pubfare since it's in Berkeley

1989: 350 barrels
1990: 700 barrels

BOULDER CREEK BREWING
13040 Highway 9
Boulder Creek 95006   408-338-7882

President: Steve Wyman
Brewers: Mike Fisher, Hugh Weiler

Boulder Creek is a small town on Highway 9 south of San Francisco in the Santa Cruz Mountains between Santa Cruz and Santa Clara. The community is at the entrance to Big Basin Park where tourism has replaced the logging industry.

Boulder Creek Brewing is two brewers -- Mike Fisher and Hugh Weiler -- and restaurateurs Nancy Long and Steve Wyman who have paired foods and beers with a 35 item menu that includes seafood, vegetarian dishes, and steak as well as 19 selections from the pub menu.

The brewpub resembles a turn-of-the-century saloon with natural wood bar and frosted glass panels dividing the restaurant from the pub. Live music is featured Thursday through Saturday evenings.

Boulder Creek Wheat Bock - dark, sweet ale
Tall Tale Pale Ale - light amber pale ale
Redwood Ale
Lorenzo Logger Lager
1990: N/A

BREWPUB ON THE GREEN
3350 Stevenson Blvd
Fremont 94538   415-651-5510

President: John Rennels
Brewmaster: Sean Donnelly

Another first for California, Brewpub-on-the-Green, was the first microbrewery on a golf course. It was opened in September 1988 in the east Bay community of Fremont by John Rennels, a former banker and financier who became intrigued by the brewpub revolution and took a fermentation science course at UC-Davis. He teamed with Bill Owens and the two built Brewpub-on-the-Green.. Rennels persuaded Narsai David, a well-known San Francisco food personality, to come up with a menu suitable for his beers.

Brewpub menu: pubfare.

Light
California Amber
Mission Peak Porter
1989: 120 barrels
1990: 1,800 barrels

BUFFALO BILL'S BREWPUB
1082 B Street
Hayward   94541   415-886-9823
President/Brewer: Bill Owens
Equipment: Used dairy equipment, refabricated tanks and vessels.

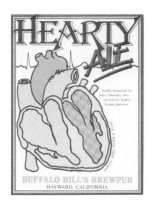

Bill Owens is a microbrewing institution. Not only did he open the second brewpub in California in September 1983, but he also started the Brew-Pac political action committe, publishes *American Brewer* magazine, and serves as unofficial spokesman of the microbrewing movement. Owens was a partner in two other Bay-area brewpubs: Bison in Berkeley and Brewpub-on-the Green in Fremont. He is currently raising money to start another brewpub and bottling operation in Hayward. One of Owens' investors is movie producer Tim Burton who used Owens' photography book, *Suburbia*, for his movie, "Edward Scissorhands."

Owens publishes *American Brewer* from an editorial office upstairs. The magazine is written with a breezy, hip style that makes it fun reading for keeping up-to-date on North American microbreweries. Features include Hot Trub gossip, news in brief, and Owens' BillSpeak column posturing on the glories and failures of microbrewing. You'll love its irreverence.

Owens brews specialty beers for historical occasions (the 50th anniversary of the Golden Gate Bridge) and healthful appeals (Hearty Ale). Owens is so proud of his Pumpkin Ale that he published the recipe, which he said was inspired by George Washington, for a column in *American Brewer*.

Brewpub menu: pubfare

Buffalo Bill's Lager
1989: 375 barrels
1990: 330 barrels

GOLDEN PACIFIC BREWERY
5515 Doyle Street
Emeryville   94608   415-547-8270
President/Brewer: David Harnden

Founded in 1985, Golden Pacific produces draft beer for Berkeley taverns and restaurants and recently installed a new bottling line.

Golden Pacific is arranging to contract brew Thousand Oaks products after the family-owned Berkeley microbrewery, one of the first in the country, ceased operations in 1989.

1989: 200 barrels
1990: N/A

GORDON BIERSCH BREWERY #1
640 Emerson
Palo Alto   94301   415-323-7723

Co-Owners: Dean Biersch, Dan Gordon
Brewmaster: Tom Davis
Equipment: Nerb Engineering, Freising West Germany

Dan Gordon and Dean Biersch have begun a two-man crusade to build brewpubs in Northern California. In three years they opened their first in Palo Alto, a second in San Jose, and plan a third for San Francisco's Embarcadero area.

Gordon-Biersch's Palo Alto brewpub is in a well-to-do downtown shopping area near the Stanford University campus. The brewpub's casual atmosphere appeals to affluent professionals working for the computer, high-tech, and electronics companies thriving in the Silicon Valley. The brewpub's clientele runs from mid-20 to mid-40 year-old professionals with men out numbered women about five to one on hot, summer evenings. The brewery is visible behind glass at the back of the brewpub.

Gordon-Biersch's Palo Alto brewpub has been labeled by the media as a New Age restaurant because of its menu, fashionably attired staff, handsome decor, and distinctive beers. Reception by the food press and customers has been enthusiastic, possibly portending a mini-empire of Gordon-Biersch operations throughout the Bay area.

Brewpub menu: lunches and dinners with appetizers, salads and desserts.

Export

Marzen - light, malty taste with slightly dry, hoppy finish; dark amber color

Dunkle - slightly dry, but malty, smooth taste

1989: 1,400 barrels

1990: 1,650 barrels

GORDON- BIERSCH BREWERY #2
33 East San Fernando
San Jose   95113   408-294-6785

Co-Owners: Dan Gordon, Dean Biersch
Brewmaster: Patrick Flaherty
Equipment: JV Northwest

After the success of their Palo Alto brewpub, Dan Gordon and Dean Biersch opened their second operation in downtown San Jose. They were fortunate enough to take over the Biers Brasserie brewpub that fell on hard times after only six months in business.

San Jose's city fathers were thrilled at Gordon-Biersh's appearance because it spruced up the depressed downtown area. Gordon and Biersch added $400,000 to the existing $1.5 million Biers Brasserie before opening in the spring of 1990. One addition was an outdoor dining area.

Brewmaster Dan Gordon is a graduate of the five-year brewery engineering program at the Weihenstephan Technical Institute in Munich. His brewing specialty is German-style beers brewed according to the Reinheitsgebot purity law. Biersch's background is in food management with Hilton hotels. He oversees the food operations in the two Gordon-Biersch brewpubs.

Brewpub menu: lunches and dinners featuring chicken skewers, black beans, salsa, Bavarian pork plates, sausages, cheeses and desserts

1989: N/A

1990: N/A

HUTTENHAIN'S BENICIA BREWING
321 First Street #5
Benicia 94510   707-747-9000
Co-owners: Tod Huttenhain, Phil Huttenhain

J & L BREWING
1945 San Francisco Boulevard, Suite # F
San Rafael   94901   415-459-4846
President: Jim Hyde

LIND BREWING
1933 Davis Street #177
San Leandro   94577   415-562-0866
President/Brewmaster: Roger Lind
Equipment: JV Northwest, used dairy equipment and English
cellar tanks

Roger Lind has made the brewpub circuit around the Bay area, having worked in Berkeley's Triple Rock and Golden Gate Breweries and Walnut Creek's Devil Mountain brewpub until he raised money to start his own brewery in the Marin County community of San Leandro. Lind's one-man warehouse operation currently is the Bay area's smallest commercial microbrewery.

Lind delivered his first batch of kegged Sir Francis Stout to area brewpubs and restaurants in the fall of 1989. He conducts tours by appointment when he isn't brewing, scrubbing floors, or delivering beer. He plans to expand in his spacious warehouse.

Lind's beers are cold-filtered, unpasteurized draft ales sold only in kegs.

Sir Francis Stout - dark, hoppy, high-alcohol and full-bodied
Captain's Porter - smooth, dark porter with taste of chocolate
Drake's Gold - crisp, golden ale brewed with Oregon Cascade hops
Drake's Ale - reddish English-style bitter with good balance

1989: 42 barrels
1990: 450 barrels

MARIN BREWING
1809 Larkspur Landing Circle
Larkspur 94939   415-461-4677

President/Brewmaster: Brendan Moylan
Equipment: Lowell & Co.; Dr. Michael Lewis consultant

Brendan Moylan opened his brewpub near the Larkspur Ferry waterfront in Marin County where commuters daily sail back and forth across the Bay into San Francisco.

Moylan and fellow brewer Grant Johnston were award-winning brewers after studying with Dr. Michael Lewis at the UC-Davis. Moylan and Johnston make a half dozen hand-crafted ales with more planned to suit requests for the exotic.

Brewpub menu: pizzas, soups, salads, sandwiches

Marin Weisse
Hefe Weisse - unfiltered version of the Marin Weisse
Mt. Tam Pale Ale - a golden ale
Albion Amber Ale - medium bodied amber ale
Point Reyes Porter - sweet, dark porter brewed with eight malts
San Quentin Breakout Stout - rich, stong, black-as-coal stout which won a gold medal at the 1989 Great American Beer Festival
Old Dipsea Barley Wine - brewed with seven malts to produce high alcohol after-dinner beer

1989: 710 barrels
1990: 1,265 barrels

PACIFIC COAST BREWING
906 Washington Street
Oakland 94607   415-836-BREW

President: Steve Wolff
Brewer: Don Gortemiller
Equipment: Former Palo Alto Brewery equipment from Inn Brewing

Pacific Coast was the first brewery that opened in Oakland since the Pacific Brewery closed in 1959. And it was the city's first brewpub to open since

PACIFIC COAST BREWING CO.

Prohibition. The 100-seat brewpub is in the renovated Old Oakland downtown district. The decor is antique saloon, complete with the hand-carved bar and stained glass from the old Cox Saloon on permanent loan from the Oakland Museum. Owners Steve Wolff and Don Gortemiller were college roommates at Berkeley in 1975 when Wolff gave Gortemiller, a chemistry student, a homebrew kit for a birthday present. Gortemiller became an avid homebrewer and applied his chemistry background to learn the intricacies of fermentation science. Wolff and Gortemiller later joined with Barry Lazurus and the three friends opened their brewery in October 1988.

Pacific Coast sponsors seminars on beer, pub crawls, and tastings. In addition to carrying four of their own beers, Pacific Coast has 15 California microbrewed beers on tap and brews several seasonal beers during the year.

The downstairs brewery in their 114-year old Victorian building is visible through a glass floor. A beer garden is planned for the future.

Brewpub menu: pubfare, salads, sandwiches

Gray Whale Ale - medium body amber ale
Blue Whale Ale - full bodied, copper colored, hoppy but slightly sweet
Killer Whale Stout - creamy, smooth, with roasted coffee taste

1989: 268 barrels
1990: 400 barrels

PETE'S BREWING COMPANY
514 High Street
Palo Alto   94301   415-328-7383

President: Mark Bozini
Brewmaster: Pete Slosberg
Equipment: Contract brewer

Pete Slosberg was an electronics marketing executive when he developed an interest in home brewing. In 1986 he began contract brewing at the Palo Alto Brewery, then switched to the August Schell Brewery in New Ulm, Minnesota, when Palo Alto closed.

At the 1987 Great American Beer Festival, Pete's Wicked Ale was voted one of the Best Beers in America. At the time, Slosberg had a picture of his dog (who bore a striking resemblance to Budweiser's Spuds Mackenzie) on the label.

After his initial burst of glory, Slosberg tried to capitalize on his success but had problems with limited capital and a failing Palo Alto Brewery. Slosberg brought in Mark Bozini and Alan Shapiro from Seagrams as president and sales manager in 1989. Bozini and Shapiro had different ideas on selling specialty beers in a fiercely competitive market. Slosberg's new partners redesigned the product, packaging, and marketing program (Pete's dog on the label was an early casualty) with healthy amounts of venture capital and new investors.

Pete's Brewing, which is still contracting with August Schell, has begun marketing two new beers -- Pacific Dry and Gold Coast Lager -- in select markets in 25 states.

Pete's Wicked Ale - brewed with pale, crystal and chocolate malts and Cascade hops; amber-colored, malty, sweet in English brown ale tradition
Pete's Pacific Dry
Pete's Gold Coast Lager

1989: 5,000 barrels
1990: 11,700 barrels

SAN FRANCISCO BREWING
155 Columbus Avenue
San Francisco   94133   415-434-3344
President/Brewer: Allan Paul
Equipment: Zaft constructed handmade copper brewkettle

Allan Paul, an award-winning homebrewer, started San Francisco's first brewpub in 1986 in the old Albatross Saloon whose origin dated to the turn of the century. San Francisco's stained glass windows, mahogany bar, large bar clock, and "oompah" fans lend an authentic, classic saloon effect.

San Francisco Brewing is in the old Barbary Coast section of town, a short walk from the financial district, Chinatown, North Beach and Union Square. City Lights Bookstore, a popular city landmark, is a block away on Columbus Avenue.

Paul hired two San Francisco craftsmen -- coopersmith Fred Zaft and designer Robert McAndrews -- to design and build his brewery, which is

behind glass on the corner of Columbus and Pacific Avenues. The three-vessel system has the capacity to brew 1,000 barrels annually.

Mayor Diane Feinstein attended San Francisco Brewing's grand opening in 1986 and Paul was featured in an August 1987 *Newsweek* article.

Brewpub menu: pubfare

Albatross Lager *- a golden pilsener*

Emperor Norton Lager *- an amber lager named after San Francisco's eccentric*

Emporer

Gripman's Porter

1989: 826 barrels
1990: 850 barrels

TIED HOUSE CAFE AND BREWERY
954 Villa Street
Mountain View 94041   415-965-BREW
President: Lou Jemison
Brewers: Bob Stoddard, Chuck Tom

The Tied House is in a 1920s building in downtown Mountain View that has been remodeled with open space, high ceilings, large windows, and a trellised beer garden. The brewpub's name refers to the old custom of breweries owning taverns and making them a "tied house" selling exclusively products from the brewery.

The brewpub's principals include several professionals in the beverage and restaurant industries. Owner Lou Jemison was in restaurant management for many years and has a farm in Monterey Bay where produce for the brewpub is grown. Brewers Chuck Tom and Bob Stoddard were involved in the Palo Alto Brewery before it went out of business in 1988. General Manager Charles O'Neill is a graduate of the Cornell School of Hotel Administration and worked at California hotels and resorts. Executive chef Emerson DeLucia has international restaurant experience. Tied House's clientele is upscale computer and electronics professionals from Silicon Valley communities.

Tied House's 20 barrel brewery has the capability of producing 3,800 barrels a year. Management claims this gives Tied House the largest brewery production for on-site consumption in the country. In 1989, Tied House brewed the second largest production for brewpubs in the U.S.

Tied House's second brewpub is scheduled to open in late 1991 in the historic San Pedro Square of downtown San Jose, home of two other microbreweries.

Brewpub menu: complete lunches and dinners

Tied House Pale

Tied House Amber

Tied House Dark - *a double wheat (Doppleweizen); double the amount of hops balanced with wheat malt*

Anndex Stout

Tied House Ginger

1989: 1,976 barrels
1990: 2,400 barrels

TRIPLE ROCK BREWERY
1920 Shattuck Avenue
Berkeley 94704   415-843-2739

Co-owners: John & Reid Martin
Brewer: Rich Warner
Equipment: JV Northwest

Triple Rock has been a success since it was first opened by John and Reid Martin near the Berkeley campus in 1986. The Martins changed the original name from Roaring Rock after a Pennsylvania brewery advised them that there might be a trademark problem with their popular Rolling Rock beer that could take years to resolve in the courts.

Triple Rock is in a modest storefront building that used to be a shoe store. The brewkettle is visible from the sidewalk and the rest of the equipment is squeezed into a narrow space all the way to the back of the building. Triple Rock is busy almost every day and night with Berkeley students, tourists, locals, and beer lovers from all over the Bay area. A small beer garden on the roof takes care of the spillover during warm weather.

The Martins have been so successful that they have started a small chain of brewpubs with a casual but funky atmosphere. They have already opened two more brewpubs, Big Time in Seattle near the University of Washington campus , and 20 Tank south of Market Street in San Francisco.

Brewpub menu: pubfare

Pinnacle Pale Ale - amber ale, mildly hoppy
Red Rock Ale - coppery red ale
Black Rock Porter - medium heavy, dark roasted malt flavor

1989: 1,550 barrels
1990: 1,700 barrels

TWENTY TANK BREWERY
316 11th Street
San Francisco 94103   415-255-9455
President: John Martin
Brewers: Rick Warner & Pete Leavitt

Twenty Tank is the third brewpub developed by the Martin family which has had success with Berkeley's Triple Rock and Seattle's Big Time, both campus brewpubs. Their latest creation is south of Market in downtown San Francisco near the Paradise Lounge, the Oasis and Slims nightclubs.

A three-dimensional neon beer mug and brick facade greet patrons entering Twenty Tank. Its warehouse setting features high ceilings, tin walls, exposed beams, and open spaces accomodating the brewery's 20 tanks in the rear.

Twenty Tank's clientele is a mixture of Berkeley (and Triple Rock) alumni, nightclub patrons, late-night carousers, brewpub regulars, and rock music fans. The attractive posters on the walls were designed by Berkeley artist Barbara Flores and recall the colorful posters of years past, featuring scantily clad bar maids in alluring poses balancing trays of beer.

Brewpub menu: pubfare

Mellow Flow Pale Ale
Hi Top Ale
Kinnikinick Amber Ale
Kinnikinick Stout

1990: 720 barrels (opened September 7)

WINCHESTER BREWING
830 S. Winchester Boulevard
San Jose   95128   408-243-7561

President: Tamerlane D. Sanchez
Brewer: Roger Gribble
Equipment: Western Brewing System

The Freshest Beer and Finest Food

San Jose's first brewpub, the Winchester Brewery, opened on June 11, 1988. Owner Tamerlane Sanchez is a former master goldsmith and homebrewer who raised $800,000 from his family to start the brewpub. A private collection of brewing memorabilia is on display.

Winchester is a casual, family-style brewpub with a 115-seat capacity in a 4,400 sq. ft. facility. Future plans include expansion to a 30-barrel system designed by L & L Fabricators. Expansion will allow for distributing Winchester's ales in the Sacramento Valley.

San Jose's Winchester Mystery House is 1 1/2 block away from the brewpub.

Brewpub menu: appetizers, seafood, sandwiches, entrees

Winchester Pale Ale - English-style bitters, honey colored
Winchester Red Ale - reddish-brown, robust and full-bodied
Winchester Porter - chestnut brown, rich and creamy
La Ve Con Cop - (tiger in Vietnamese) a light ale produced for the San Jose Asian community
1989: 600 barrels
1990: 800 barrels

NORTHERN CALIFORNIA BAY AREA

BROWN STREET BREWERY
1300 Brown Street
Napa   94559   707-255-6392
Co-Owners: Dan Holm, Dale Parker
Brewer: Dan Holm
Equipment: Pub Brewing; self-designed and constructed.

Brown Steet Brewpub is one of California's newest having opened in May 1990 a few blocks from downtown Napa. The brewpub represents the merger of freshly-made pizza and "Holm brewed" beer.

Dan Holm was in the bottling business for 24 years with Northern California wineries, soft drink, and champagne companies and wanted to start his own beverage business. After taking advanced homebrewing courses at Great Fermentations in Santa Rosa under Byron Burch, Holm made the decision to start his own brewpub.

Holm met Dale Parker who owned a Napa pizza parlor that had once been a comedy cafe. The two joined their ventures and used Dan's skill at operating a beverage facility and Parker's pizza talents. They reconfigured their building into a pizza/deli/brewpub with a couple of fresh ideas in the brewing area.

Dan brews two beers that you won't find in other Northern California brewpubs -- ginseng and chili beer. Ginseng beer is for the health food and Asian restaurant trade and tastes a little woody. Chili beer is a pilsener with a mild, malty taste for about five seconds. Then something ignites in the back of your throat like you swallowed a hot pepper! Chili beer is probably more suited to South Texas or New Mexico palates, but no one can accuse Californians of being unimaginative. It's definitely the beer to order when you're having only one, although Holm says brave customers order a pitcher and finish it in one sitting.

Brewpub menu: pubfare, pizzas

Wheat - mellow, fruity, with Nuggett, Hallertauer hops
Catskill Mountain Wild Ginseng - slightly woody, neutral taste
Brown Ale - coffee-colored, Cascade hops
Oatmeal Stout - dark, rich, nutty taste; excellent after-dinner drink
Chili Beer - pale pilsener with chili extract
Porter - light body, brown color
Pale Ale
1990: 70 barrels (opened in May 1990)

KELMERS BREWHOUSE
458 B Street
Santa Rosa   95401   707-544-4677

President: Bruce Kelm
Brewmaster: Tim O'Day
Equipment: Berkhamsted

Bruce Kelm's entry into the ranks of pub brewers is not dissimlar from other Americans who discovered real ale in England and made a career change to become a microbrewer. Kelm was a Northwestern MBA graduate working for a medical supply company in England when he first tried English ales. It didn't take long for him to get rid of his medical supply kit, return home, and start his own brewpub.

Kelm brought Irish brewer Tim O'Day with him to northern California and the two began developing a business plan. Kelm studied restaurant operations and incorporated features he thought were hallmarks of successful operations: clean bathrooms, dartboards, piped-in music, big-screen TVs, and the sports page tacked to the mens' room wall to discourage grafitti.

To produce authentic English-style ales, Kelm and O'Day purchased a wood-jacketed Berkhamsted brewing system and opened in October 1988 in downtown Santa Rosa, the county seat of Sonoma County. Kelmers is expanding wholesale distribution in Sonoma County with draft sales; a modified 750 oz. bottling line is in the works to meet the growing demand for their beers.

Bruce's wife is the daughter of John Jakes, author of popular historical novels. When Jakes' *Gold Coast* was published in 1989, Bruce brewed a special California Gold as a promotion for the book.

Brewpub menu: pubfare, lunches and dinners

Kelm's Krystal Wheat
Klassic Amber Ale
Kelm's Klout Stout

1989: 1,040 barrels
1990: 1,300 barrels

MONTEREY BREWING
638 Wave Street
Monterey 93940
408-375-3634

Owner/Brewer: Tony Bindel
Equipment: Combination of Grundy tanks, winery, dairy and custom designed equipment.

Monterey brewpub opened in 1989 on the Cannery Row waterfront made famous by John Steinbeck, who lived there during the Depression. The brewpub's atmosphere is, not surprisingly, waterfront bar complete with dart board, small dance floor, and jukebox. Wave Street is a touristy area with restaurants, taverns, T-shirt and souvenir shops.

Monterey's original 22 oz. bottles have been replaced by 740 ml. and 12 oz. bottles for off-premise trade. Although it has limited production, Monterey's beers are sold throughout Bay area outlets.

Brewpub menu: pubfare

Save the Whale Pale Ale - IPA ale brewed with Cascade hops
Amber
Sea Lion Stout

1989: 98 barrels
1990: 300 barrels

NAPA VALLEY BREWING/ CALISTOGA INN
1250 Lincoln Avenue
Calistoga 94515 707-942-4101

President: Ken Nilsson
Brewer: Todd Scott
Equipment: L & L Fabricators; Dr. Michael Lewis and Steve Hambly consultants.

Calistoga is a picturesque village at the north end of the Napa Valley -- an area noted for spas, wineries, and beautiful vineyards. In this scenic area, Phil Rogers, a former Air Force bomber pilot and trained chef, converted a turn-of-the-century Calistoga Inn into a brewpub. Calistoga's first beer was poured during Thanksgiving 1987. Rogers sold the Calistoga Inn in 1989 and moved to

Seattle to open another brewpub, Duwamps Cafe and Seattle Brewing (see Northwest section.)

At one time the Napa Valley was a perfect place for growing hops because of its arid weather and rich soil. Today, tourists drive north from San Francisco to visit wineries and shop. At the north end of the scenic Napa Valley is the quiet town of Calistoga.

Guests at the 17-room Calistoga Inn receive a complimentary half-pint of fresh ale from the brewery or a glass of Napa Valley wine. Chef Leo Kleinhanz' menu has received high ratings from restaurant critics; his specialties are lamb, poultry, and veal cooked over a hardwood fire.

There are few more charming spots in Northern California to enjoy a fresh beer than the patio of the Calistoga Inn. A creek meanders below and a vine-covered trellis shades diners from the afternoon sun. Birds and butterflies fly around the bubbling fountain and breezes cool the air, even during the mid-summer heat.

The Calistoga Inn's water tower was converted by Rogers into the brewery. The brewery's second floor houses the mill; the ground floor serves as the brewhouse and serving cellar. The inn is a short walk from Calistoga's shops and boutiques.

Brewpub menu: complete lunches and dinners with special emphasis on fish, pastas, and specialty dishes.

B & B rates: moderate ($40-45/person/day)

Calistoga Lager
Beat the Heat Wheat - refreshing, light and flowery aroma; brewed with 60% wheat and Tettnanger hops
Pale Ale

1989: 300 barrels
1990: N/A

SAN ANDREAS BREWING/EARTHQUAKE COUNTY PUB
737 San Benito Street
Hollister 95023 408-637-7074
President: Bill Millar

Some might think it's too cute to be brewing in Hollister on top of the San Andreas geological fault and marketing Earthquake Pale and Seismic Ale. But Bill Millar was prescient when he came out with Oktoberquake beer for his Fall 1989 specialty beer. On October 17, northern California was jolted by the

Loma Prieta earthquake, the worst in decades. About one-third of the buildings in Hollister were damaged beyond repair.

San Andreas Brewing, however, survived only a few cracks and fallen plaster. A 1,000 gallon batch was lost when the electricity failed while the brew was in the fermentation vats. "Of course the place filled up afterwards," Millar recalls. The crowd wasn't seeking shelter; rather, they were taking advantage of Millar's policy of serving nickel drafts during a tremor!

Millar opened on September 22, 1988 in the old Baywood Creamery, salvaging the original creamery stools for the bar. His beers are all top-fermented: two amber ales, a pale ale, a porter, and specialties cherry ale and apricot ale. San Andreas products are available on draft and in 22 oz. bottles.

Brewpub menu: pubfare and seafood dishes, including catfish, shark, and calamari deep-fried in beer batter

Earthquake Pale - brewed with crystal malt and a mixture of domestic (Cascade, Chinook) and German (Tettnanger) hops; tart, citrus taste up front reminds one of a wheat beer, but this is more highly hopped

Seismic Ale - light amber ale brewed with Munich and crystal malt and a blend of Cascade, Chinook, Cluster and Goldings hops

Kit Fox Amber - malty, red amber named after an endangered species of local mammal

Earthquake Porter - brewed with a mixture of roasted barley, pale, crystal and chocolate malts

1989: 500 barrels
1990: 1,500 barrels

SANTA CRUZ BREWING/FRONT STREET PUB
516 Front Street
Santa Cruz 95060   408-429-8838
Owner: Gerald J. Turgeon
Brewer: Scott Morgan

Santa Cruz Brewery, one of the first Northern California brewpubs, is two miles from the beach on busy Front Street. The town is a popular beach resort two hours southwest of San Francisco. Crowds jam the town every spring and summer weekend to enjoy the sun, sand, surf, and suds.

The Front Street Brewpub decor is nautical with blonde wood, shake roof over the bar, and a working lighthouse light above. Reproductions of West Coast lighthouses hang on the wall and a wooden facade from an abandoned Coast Guard lighthouse adjoins the brewery in the back. As one might expect, the brewpub's clientele runs heavily to the beach crowds in the summer and students from Santa Cruz University during the fall and winter. Live entertainment including bluegrass groups play on Saturday nights.

Santa Cruz is on the San Andreas faultline and during the October 17, 1989 Loma Prieta earthquake, tremors devastated bars and restaurants along Front Street. The Front Street Brewpub was a casualty for two weeks, but reopened and reportedly business has resumed to pre-quake levels.

Brewpub menu: pubfare

Lighthouse Lager - pale straw color, dry pilsener-style

Amber - honey colored, slight caramel taste

Stout - black, slightly sweet

1989: 1,455 barrels
1990: N/A

SEABRIGHT BREWERY
519 Seabright Avenue
Santa Cruz   95062   408-426-2739
Co-Owners: Charlie Meehan, Keith Cranmer
Brewer: Richard Young
Equipment: 7 barrel JV Northwest system

Charlie Meehan and Keith Cranmer, boyhood friends in upstate New York, followed each other around the country until they both ended up in California. Cranmer was in the rodeo belt engraving business in Berkeley and Meehan was a Santa Cruz contractor when they decided to go into the brewpub business in the mid-1980s. Relying on Meehan's contractor experience, they opened Seabright brewpub on May

14, 1988 only four months after they acquired the property. Seabright cost approximately $400,000 to open.

A survey found that Seabright's street corner is the busiest intersection in Santa Cruz county with more that 57,000 cars passing by every day. Nevertheless, many of the clientele walk to Seabright from adjoining neighborhoods. After the 1989 earthquake, the neighborhood became a peninsula when it was cut off from bridge traffic. Seabright became even more popular when locals were stranded for several days. According to Cranmer, sales went up 30%.

An attractive feature of Seabright is the patio where clientele lunch in the afternoon and linger in the evening. The beach is a five-minute walk away and sailers from the yacht club stroll up for a couple of fresh beers after a hard day of sailing. Brewpub regulars include crews from as far away as San Diego.

The decor is predominantely pastel greens, blues and greys. The atmosphere is casual, with most clientele wearing T-shirts, sandals and shorts.

Brewpub menu: contemporary American bistro cuisine. Chef Douglas Gruen's recipe for chili simmered in stout won first prize at the Santa Cruz Chili Cook-off in 1989.

Baxter's Best - *malty, smooth dark amber, slightly bitter aftertaste*
Seabright Amber - *smooth, malty taste similar to English mild*
Pelican Pale - *light, smooth lager*
Gales Ale - *amber colored*

1989: 681 barrels
1990: N/A

STANISLAUS BREWERY AND BREWPUB
821 L Street
Modesto 95354   209-524-2337

President/Brewmaster: Garith Helm
Equipment: Mueller tanks, Siminozzi bottling line, and various hand-built systems

Garith Helm and his wife Romy began thinking about turning a homebrewing hobby into a commercial venture in early 1980s. when Helm was working as an engineer at Lawrence Livermore Lab.

The Helms began Stanislaus brewery in the Central Valley town of Modesto with initial production limited to 1,000 barrels/year. Their packaging progressed from kegs, to liter bottles, beer balls, and finally into conventional 12-oz. bottles. St. Stan's specialties are German-style alt beers brewed with top fermenting yeast at lagering temperatures. Romy introduced Garith to these unique beers on trips to her home in Dusseldorf, Germany.

Stanislaus has fun with its image as the local offbeat brewery with its own "saint." St. Stans is actually Director of Marketing Rueben Torch, a retired professor who dons clerical robes to officiate at brewery functions. St. Stans blesses the beer as a quality control measure with proper Latin incantations and has been known to perform miracles such as walking on beer.

In honor of hometown boy George Lucas whose movie "American Graffiti" was filmed in Modesto, Stanislaus brewed Graffiti beer in 1989 with a 1957 Corvette on the label. The bottling sold out within a week but Stanislaus is planning future bottlings with classic American cars on the label.

Stanislaus' production capacity was limited to 3,000 barrels/year at its original location in a shed at the Helms' home on Shoemake Avenue. The Helms raised $3 million to build a new brewery and brewpub in downtown, which opened October 12, 1990. The new Stanislaus brewery/brewpub includes an outdoor beer garden, tasting room, gift shop, and clock tower with a likeness of St. Stans on the door. Capacity at the new location is 12,000 barrels a year with room to expand to 24,000 barrels.

St. Stan's beers are featured at Disney World and have received excellent ratings from California publications.

St. Stan's Alt Bier - fermented with top fermenting yeast but at lagering temperatures to produce a slightly sweet, hoppy but smooth beer

St. Stan's Amber
St. Stan's Dark
St. Stan's Fest

1989: 3,000 barrels
1990: 3,125 barrels

WILLETT'S BREWING
902 Main Street
Napa   94559   707-258-2337

President: Charles Willett Ankeny
Brewer: Brian W. Hunt
Equipment: Combination of British ageing tanks and locally designed and constructed mash tun

Napa means wineries and vineyards in California but in 1989 in the heart of Napa wine country, Brian Hunt and Charles Ankeny started a brewpub. Hunt had been a brewer for 10 years and Ankeny is the great-grandson of Theodore Hamm, the founder of the Hamm's brewery in Minnesota.

Willett's Brewery is located in a former restaurant at a bend in the Napa River adjacent to a city park. Hunt and Ankeny built an outdoor beer garden in the summer of 1989. Patrons now can sit inside a dining room looking out over the Napa River or enjoy the scenery from outside. The brewpub is across the street from the county courthouse and is a popular lunch place with lawyers and court clerks. Willett's patio at the end of 2nd Street was leased at a modest cost after it was declared surplus property by the city as an abandoned public right-of-way.

Chef Greg Cole has a number of dishes from mini-pizzas to steamed mussels that are well-complimented by Willett's beers. Brewer Hunt chooses from 16 recipes for the four beers on tap. A few Napa taverns also carry Willett's beer on draft. Brewery capacity is 1,000 barrels/year.

Willetts cost approximately $450,000 to open; a second brewpub is planned for Colorado and a third in the Northern California.

Brewpub menu: complete lunches and dinners

Full Moon Light Ale

Willy's Lager - flowery, light pilsener

Victory Ale - dark, creamy, mellow,

Nelson's Black Beer - coffee-colored, sweet and mellow (named after Nelson Mandela)

Golden Thistle Bitter Ale

Old Magnolia Stout

1989: 600 barrels
1990: 750 barrels

NORTHERN CALIFORNIA

North Coast and Inland

ANDERSON VALLEY BREWING
14081 Highway 128
Boonville 95415   707-895-2337

President: Kenneth Allen
Brewer: William Harper
Equipment: Various sources in U.S., Britain, New Zealand

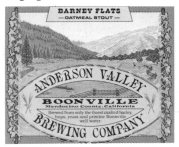

In an earlier era, Anderson Valley was a Mendocino County logging community about 2 1/2 hours north of San Francisco. In the picturesque valley where sheep graze among apple orchards, locals keep alive the local dialect called "boontling." The rugged countryside was isolated until the state built a highway inland from the coast a few years ago.

Ken and Kimberly Allen opened Anderson Valley in Boonville (pop. 1,500) in 1987. Ken had been a Boonville chiropractor for 20 years and felt he needed a career change. He began brewing in 1985 in the back of his office and opened the brewpub and gift shop in the old Buckhorn Saloon, built in 1873.

Buckhorn's windows look westward on meadows and hills just a few miles from the coast. The picturesque scene from the Buckhorn is duplicated on Anderson Valley's labels.

Anderson Valley's beers are named after the colorful folklore of the region: Boont Amber is named for the Boontling community; High Rollers Wheat for the gateway region to Anderson Valley; Deep Enders for the citizens of the Iteville area; and Poleeko Gold for the "Polleekers" who wore bluejay feathers in their hat bands. Anderson Valley's beers have developed a strong and well-deserved following in the San Francisco area; they are exceptionally well-brewed.

Anderson Valley also brews specialty beers for draft accounts including a Centennial (for every 100 brews), a summer Whamber (wheat bock), Winter Solstice, and an ESB.

Brewpub menu: pubfare, salads, sandwiches and dinner entrees.

Boont Amber Ale - pale ale, cooper-colored, distinctive
High Rollers Wheat - crisp and light; a summer delight
Deep Enders Dark - a smooth and tasty porter
Poleeko Gold - a light ale
Barney Flats Oatmeal Stout - rich, sweet and mellow

1989: 900 barrels
1990: 1,350 barrels

BACK ALLEY BREWERY
5219 Glide
Davis   95616   916-753-4571
Co-owners: Al Geitner, Michael Lewis
Brewer: Brad Nesbitt
Equipment: Pub Brewing

The Davis Back Alley Brewpub was inevitable -- it's the location of the Department of Fermentation Science at the University of California and home of Dr. Michael Lewis, who is head of the department. Lewis is one of the leading figures in microbrewing and has developed a career as brewing consultant and designer of microbrewing systems. Lewis teamed with Al Geitner, who had a long career in the beverage industry, to form the Pub Brewing Company.

Back Alley is a campus tavern with spacious main room, wooden tables and booths, pool table, cement floor, dart board and a row boat suspended upside-down over the bar. The L-shaped bar allows anyone sitting at the bar to watch brewing behind the enclosed glass partition.

Back Alley has the Wurlitzer-style jukebox loaded with old tunes for aging hippies and nostalgia-minded students. Old 45s include classics by Gladys Knight and the Pips, Billy Ocean, Janis Joplin, Mitch Ryder, Chubby Checker, Manfred Mann, the Turtles, Rod Stewart, Marvin Gaye, Three Dog Night, CCR, and the Kinks. One can only imagine how many generations of future Davis students will learn about English-style ales and old time rock-and-roll in the Back Alley brewpub.

The Back Alley campus pub atmosphere is contrasted with the German-style beer hall at Sudwerks brewpub five minutes away. The two represent the range of brewpubs that can prosper together, even in a medium-sized community like Davis.

Brewpub menu: pubfare
1990: (opened May)

DEAD CAT ALLEY BREWERY
667 Dead Cat Alley
Woodland   95695   916-661-1521
President/Brewer: Jim Schleuter
Equipment: Self-designed and locally constructed

Dead Cat Alley Brewpub is located on the main street of Woodland, a bedroom community for Sacramento 15 miles away along Interstate 5. Jim Schleuter originally built the River City Brewery and Hogshead Brewpub in Sacramento during the mid-1980s.

Dead Cat's equipment is in three locations, brew kettle and mash tun in the rear, fermentation tanks in the back hallway, and serving tanks behind the bar. Most of the 7 barrel stainless steel system is contained in square wooden boxes designed by Schleuter. A small bottling operation is run from the fermentation room.

The clientele consists of locals who come in to watch big screen TV, play video games, throw darts, and drink fresh beer.

Brewpub menu: pubfare

Dead Cat Lager
Cat Tail Ale
Fat Cat Stout

1989: 470 barrels
1990: 700 barrels

ETNA BREWERY
131 Callahan
Etna 96207   916-467-5277

Owner/Brewer: Andrew Hurlimann
Equipment: Tri-City Brewery equipment from Kennewick, Washington

Etna is southeast of Yreka in picturesque Scott Valley where it looks like time has stood still for 100 years. It is surrounded by mountains and snowy

Mount Shasta towers in the east. Scott Valley is about 50 miles long with green pastures, cattle ranches, orchards, red barns, and acres of alfalfa and hay.

One hundred year-old Etna is two blocks long and three blockswide. The museum (open 1-3 PM on weekdays) is under the care of the Golden Daughters of the Golden West. Museum artifacts include pictures, maps, clothing, tools from early settlers, and a bottle from the original Etna Brewery.

Rancher Andy Hurlimann is another young brewer (32 years old) reviving the tradition of small town Western breweries. Hurlimann received an industrial technology degree at Chico State and spent time at Sierra Nevada learning brewing. He began homebrewing and won awards at local and national homebrew shows.

After Chico State and a stint at Sierra Nevada, Hurlimann returned home to Etna (pop. 800) south of the Oregon border with the idea of starting a microbrewery. He bought property in 1987 and worked three years to build his brewery on the site of the original Etna Brewery. The previous Etna brewery was run by the Kappler family from the 1870s until it closed in 1920 at the advent of Prohibition. At the turn of the century during the gold mining days, the Etna Brewery was making $250,000 a year.

The Etna microbrewery is in a new building one block from Main Street and across from a cattle pasture. Hurlimann adapted the original Etna Brewery label and put up old photos of the brewery around the building. He began brewing in the summer of 1990.

Hurliman sells three beers locally and self-distributes 22 oz. bottles and kegs to Yreka and around Siskiyou County. He believes he is related to the family which owns the Hurlimann brewery in Switzerland.

Etna Ale
Etna Dark Lager
Etna Export
1990: 50 barrels

HOGSHEAD BREWERY
114 J Street
Sacramento   95814   916-443-2739
President/Brewer: Phil Salmon
Equipment: Custom designed by Jim Schleuter

Hogshead was the second brewery started by Jim Schleuter who began with Sacramento's River City Microbrewery and moved to the Dead Cat Brewpub in Woodland after Hogshead. The downstairs brewpub is located in the touristy Old Sacramento that recreates the theme of California of years gone by.

Hogshead's clientele is mostly locals who come in to play pool, listen to the jukebox, eat pizza and drink beer. The brewing equipment designed by Schleuter is located in three separate areas.

Brewpub menu: pubfare, pizzas

Hogshead Pale Ale
McSchlueter Dark Ale
Hogshead Lager

1989: 600 barrels
1990: 1,400 barrels

HUMBOLDT BREWERY
856 10th Street
Arcata   95521   707-826-2739
President: Mario Celotto
Brewer: John DeMarinis

Not all pro athletes turn to pitching Miller Lite when their playing days are over. Mario Celotto, former linebacker for the Oakland Raiders, bought himself a brewpub. Humboldt Brewery in downtown Arcata is, not surprisingly, decorated with memorabilia from Celotto's career and is equipped with a large screen TV for viewing Raiders games.

Brewmaster John DeMarinis serves a repertoire of four English ales (including an award-winning oatmeal stout), with occasional seasonal specialties. All are fermented two weeks, then placed in cold storage for a month before being pumped to the bar via traditional English handpumps or "beer engines." The aging and storing tanks are visible behind the bar.

The brewpub is at the back of the building that also has a dining room with a stone fireplace. In 1990, Celotto leased the adjoining facility which includes a dance hall for concerts for performers like Kris Kristofferson touring the North Coast Country.

Brewpub menu: pubfare, fish and chips, select dishes with a Cajun accent

Gold Rush Ale - *a golden amber pale ale recommended as "perfect for the ale novitiate"*

Red Nectar Ale - *a stronger ale brewed from crystal malt and a mixture of Eroica, Cascade and Willamette hops for flowery aroma and fruity flavor*

Storm Cellar Porter - *a nutty, coffee-colored porter brewed with roasted chocolate malt*

Oatmeal Stout - *brewed with rolled oats in addition to roasted barley and crystal malts; awarded a gold medal at the 1988 GABF; recommended as a dessert beer to complement the cream cheese apple cake*

1989: 1,025 barrels
1990: 1,300 barrels

LOST COAST BREWERY
617 Fourth Street
Eureka   95501   707-445-4480

Co-owners: Barbara Groom, Wendy Pound
Brewer: Barbara Groom

Lost Coast is one of California's newest brewpubs, having opened in July 1990. It is located in the old Knights of Pythias Castle on the main street of Eureka, a logging and fishing community on the northwest coast. The Redwoods National Forest is an hour north on Highway 101.

Founders Barbara Groom, a pharmacist, and Wendy Pound, a family counselor, left San Francisco to start new careers. Both took brewing classes at UC-Davis and raised $800,000 with the help of a California Enterprise Zone loan.. Lost Coast is in a former furniture store in a part of Eureka undergoing redevelopment. Groom and Pound claim they are the first women in the country to own a brewery.

Lost Coast opened for business at 6:24 PM on July 13, 1990, immediately after city health officials approved its permit to brew. According to Groom, people were lined up waiting for the town's first fresh brew.

The brewpub's decor is turn-of-the-century saloon with overhead fans, wooden tables and bar, and period art. The artistic focus of the brewpub is a stunning array of colorized and enlarged photos taken by an immigrant Italian photographer during the 1920s around the Bay area. A local artist developed the photos from original glass negatives.

Brewpub menu: pubfare

Lost Coast Pale Ale
Lost Coast Porter
Lost Coast Stout
1990: (opened July)

MAD RIVER BREWING
195 Taylor Way
Blue Lake 95525   707-668-4151
President/Brewer: Bob Smith
Equipment: Used brew kettle, mash tun, fermentation tanks, bottle washer from Sierra Nevada; two "Yorkshire Square" open fermenters

Although Bob Smith was educated as a botanist and worked as an electrician, he began brewing in 1978 after he spent a week in Sonoma helping build New Albion. Smith later worked at the Sierra Nevada, Mendocino, Humboldt, and Lost Coast breweries and earned awards for his homebrewing. In September 1989, Smith formed a corporation to start his own brewery in Blue Lake, 20 miles east of Eureka on the North Coast. He raised $200,000 and established Mad River Brewery in the Blue Lake Industrial Park. The first keg of Steelhead Extra Pale Ale was sold on December, 14, 1990; four Humboldt County taverns and restaurants currently are carrying Mad River's beers on draft.

Smith added a yeast culture lab in the brewery; he plans to culture yeast and provide it to other breweries. Brewery capacity is 2,000 barrels/year. Smith plans to add up to five more beers to Mad River's portfolio.

Steelhead Extra Pale Ale

1990: (Started brewing on December 10)

MAIN STREET BREWERY
319 Main Street
Chico 95928   916-891-4502

Owner: Dewayne Saxton
Brewer: John Abbott
Equipment: Various sources

Main Street is the old Sherwood Brewpub in downtown Chico which began as a Arthurian pub with scenes of Robin Hood, his Merry Men, and Merlin the Magician painted on the wall. One of Sherwood's founders was Dewayne Saxton who started an eponymous microbrewery in his basement.

Sherwood went through management changes during 1990. A few months after new owners took over, Sherwood was sold again to a group that included Saxton. With all of those changes, a new name was needed and Sherwood became the Main Street Brewery.

Main Street has 19 beers on tap and carries a full line of bottled California microbrewed beers. The campus-oriented brewpub features live music, pool tables, and dart boards.

Brewpub menu: pubfare

1989: 56 barrels
1990: 400 barrels (closed; reopened in 1991)

MENDOCINO BREWING
13351 Hwy 101 S.
Hopland 95449   707-744-1015

President: Michael Laybourn
Brewer: Don Barkley

Hopland is 100 miles from San Francisco (44 miles from Santa Rosa) along Highway 101 in the northern end of the wine country. Although Hopland's population is only 800, it attracts thousands of tourists every year who keep B & Bs, shops and wineries busy. Mendocino County is noted for its scenery along the Russian River that flows westward into the Pacific Ocean.

Mendocino Brewing had the distinction of being the first legal brewpub in California when it opened on August 14, 1983. Since then Mendocino has become a mecca for aspiring brewers who want to see an historic landmark from the pioneering days.

Mendocino's historical position is enhanced by the fact that its original brewing equipment came from Sonoma's New Albion Brewery, the country's first start-up microbrewery. New Albion's brewer Don Barkley and Michael Lovett also made the journey from Sonoma with the equipment and Barkley found a niche as Mendocino's brewmaster. Today, Barkley is a general partner of Mendocino and well-respected member of the microbrewing community.

Co-founders Michael Laybourn and Norman Franks' interest in microbrewing came at a time when both were looking for a business to use their combined talents. Laybourn had a background in construction and design; Franks in business and management.

In an earlier life, Mendocino was the Hopvine Saloon and today retains its original atmosphere with touches such as portraits of employees on the walls and a sandbox in the beer garden. The beer garden is shaded by hop and grapevines and is popular with workers from area vineyards and wineries.

Mendocino has gone through three major expansions and there are plans to build a 100-barrel capacity brewing facility in Ukiah, north of Hopland. New Albion's equipment is enjoying retirement in a shed and awaiting its next assignment or a call from the Smithsonian Institute. Mendocino's bottling line was picked up from Sierra Nevada by way of a Christian Brothers winery. A monthly newsletter keeps customers up-to-date on brewing activities and special events at Mendocino.

Brewpub menu: pubfare

Black Hawk Stout - *a rich, mellow stout as satisfying in the summer as it is in the winter*

Blue Heron Pale Ale - *amber color, light, hoppy finish*

Red Tail Ale - *one of most popular California microbrewed beers; reddish color, slightly hoppy and smooth*

Eye of the Hawk - *award winning specialty ale*

Yuletide Porter - *Christmas beer available only at the brewpub*

1989: 5,317 barrels
1990: 9,000 barrels

NORTH COAST BREWING
444 N. Main Street
Fort Bragg   95437   707-964-2739
General Partners: Tom Allen, Mark Ruedrich, Joe Rosenthal
Brewmaster: Mark Ruedrich
Brewing equipment: Diverse sources

Fort Bragg in Mendocino County is on the coastline about a day's drive north of San Francisco. Day trippers, tourists, and families drive north along Route #1's winding coastal road or cross over from Highway 101. Either route includes orchards, wineries, farms and stands of California Redwoods.

Fort Bragg (pop. 5,000) is a logging and fishing community north of scenic Mendocino (pop. 1,100) and Albion (pop. 308). The famous Skunk Railroad takes tourists from inland Willetts to Fort Bragg, duplicating the treacherous passage early loggers took to reach the coastal Redwood forests.

General partners Tom Allen, Mark Ruedrich, and Joe Rosenthal started North Coast brewery with a modest $300,000 in 1988. The brewery was built with equipment from various sources and produces seven beers.

At one time, the North Coast brewpub was a mortuary. Brewing is done in the back room that was the "working area" of the mortuary. The brewpub's bar came from an old Eureka saloon. Restored pictures on the walls glorify Fort Bragg's early logging days. Portland beer writer Fred Eckhardt rated North Coast his favorite California microbrewery.

Brewpub menu: lunches and dinners featuring local seafood

Ruedrich's Red Seal Ale
Scrimshaw Pilsner
Old No. 38 Stout
Summerfest Ale
Oktoberfest Ale
Christmas Ale

1989: 490 barrels
1990: 750 barrels

NEVADA CITY BREWING
75 Bost Avenue
Nevada City   95959   916-265-2446
President/Brewer: Gene Downing
Equipment: Locally designed and constructed

Founder and brewer Gene Downing is a retired Air Force pilot who opened his brewery in Nevada City a few miles from Lake Tahoe. Nevada City is a carryover from California's Gold Rush days when saloons, brothels, hotels, and jails were jammed with miners spilling gold dust from their pockets. The town's population reached 16,000 at its zenith when hydraulic mining blasted gold from the mountains.

Today, Nevada City's gas-light streets are lined with modest Victorian homes where tourists flock to remember life in early days of the Bear State. The town is laid out to meet the contour of the mountains. Some houses cling to the sides of mountains on stilts.

Gene Downing helped his brother Steve open the Truckee Brewery in 1985. He enjoyed the experience so much he opened his own brewery in 1989 in an industrial area five minutes from downtown. Downing raised about $80,000 from savings, family, friends and a few investors and shares the work with his son, Keith. Together, the father-son team runs every aspect of the operation: brewing, bottling, distributing, and cleaning up at night.

The Downings hand-fill attractive but bulky 60 oz. magnum sized bottles for accounts in the San Francisco area. A six-pack of Nevada City lager or dark weighs 360 oz! This beer is, in every sense of the word, hand-crafted; every bottle that goes out the door is handled by the Downings. Although the bottling line is a single-bottling device, it accounts for 40% of Nevada City's business. Kegs of draft beer are sold to 30 accounts in Grass Valley County.

Nevada City lagers for four weeks. Several of the 13-barrel tanks have investors' names on them so they can see their money working. With his modest approach to brewing, Downing expects to be debt-free in 18 months -- an enviable position for any small business. His ambition is "to retire again" when his oldest son returns to take over the brewery.

Nevada City Gold
Nevada City Dark

1989 639 barrels.
1990 650 barrels

RUBICON BREWING
2004 Capitol Avenue
Sacramento   95814   916-448-7032

President: Ed Brown
Brewmaster: Phil Moeller
Equipment: Western Brewing Systems, Cross Distributing

Rubicon is located in a quiet, tree-lined Sacramento neighborhood near cafes, bistros and ethnic restaurants. The brewpub's clientele are largely professionals who work in government-related professions.

Ed Brown was in banking and real estate when he took a trip to England and discovered microbreweries and real ale. When he returned to the U.S., he visited microbreweries and changed careers.

Brewmaster Phil Moeller received a masters degree in Fermentation Studies from UC-Davis. He won a silver medal in 1989 at the Great American Beer Festival.

Moeller brews several seasonal beers including Winter Wheat, Winter Wheat Wine, Springbok, Ol' Mo's Porter, and "Philsner." The brewery is visible in a glass-enclosed back room.

Brewpub menu: complete lunches and dinners

Rubicon Amber Ale - *most popular beer, brewed with Munich malt, crystal and dextrin, balanced with Clusters, Cascade, Nugget and Tettnanger hops; brewed to simulate German alt beers from Dusseldorf*

Rubicon India Pale Ale - *brewed with 80% 2-row Klages malt and 20% dextrin and crystal malt, Chinook and Cascade hops*

Rubicon Summer Wheat - *brewed with 70% wheat and 30% Klages pale malt, and four hops*

1989: 930 barrels
1990: 1,500 barrels

SIERRA NEVADA BREWERY
1075 E. 20th Street
Chico   95928   916-893-3520

President: Ken Grossman

Vice President: Paul Camusi
Brewmaster: Steve Dressler
Equipment: Used German equipment

Paul Camusi and Ken Grossman began constructing Sierra Nevada in 1979 in an industrial park with used Anchor equipment and tanks scrounged from old dairies and warehouses.

Sierra Nevada started modestly and grew slowly. Almost immediately the brewery began winning awards at the Great American Beer Festival and receiving raves for their distinctive ales, porters and stouts. Camusi and Grossman increased production gradually in the 1980s: 2,900 barrels in 1984; 4,100 in 1985; 6,800 in 1986; 10,800 in 1987; and 13,900 in 1988. With this slow but steady growth they were able to attract investors to build a new brewery with an adjoining brewpub.

In the fall of 1989, Sierra Nevada moved into its showcase brewpub which is one of the most stylish in North America. It is a classic saloon with mirrors behind the mahogany bar, polished wood, plush carpets, and lithographs on the walls. No tacky posters, videos, or giant screen TVs detract from the elegance. The attractive, state-of-the-art brewery with 100-barrel copper brewkettles is visible from inside the brewpub as well as outside.

Sierra Nevada brews three times a day, seven days a week, to meet the demand for their nationally-awarded beers. In 1990, Sierra Nevada brewed their first lager, a pale bock, with plans to brew more lagers to complement their impressive line of ales.

What Camusi and Grossman have achieved belongs in textbooks on entrepreneurship. From their modest begining in a small college town, they have created one of the most successful microbreweries in North America and brewed beers that rank with the world's best.

Brewpub menu: pubfare, lunches and dinners

Sierra Nevada Pale Ale - *rich amber color, flowery hops and creamy head; wonderful aromatic head that lasts and lasts*

Sierra Nevada Porter - *dark, rich porter brewed with roasted malts to produce a dry, chocolatey flavor*

Sierra Nevada Stout - *creamy, dark and very rich*

Sierra Nevada Celebration Ale - *numerous dark malts and multiple hops produce this annual holiday treat; complex and fruity, with delightful after-tastes of holiday sweets*

Sierra Nevada Bigfoot Barleywine - *hefty, dark and rich, a well balanced barleywine, with the highest alcohol content (8.5%) of any American beer*

1989: 20,884 barrels
1990: 31,000 barrels

SUDWERK PRIVATBRAUEREI HUBSH
2001 Second Street
Davis   95616   916-758-8700
Co-Owners: Ron Broward, Dean Unger
Brewer: Karl Elden

Davis, home of the University of California extension which awards degrees in Fermentation Science, now boasts two brewpubs that coincidentally opened the same weekend in May 1990, a five-minute drive from each other.

Sudwerk Privatbrauerei Hubsch co-owners Ron Broward and Dean Unger, an architect and construction engineer respectively, spared little expense to make their brewpub an authentic German beer hall. They imported a German brewery, brass accessories, and pictures from old German breweries, but modernized with features such as motion sensitive lights, sinks, and toilets in the bathroom! Hubsch's label even looks like an German import.

Sudwerk is housed in a new building alongside Interstate 80 and designed to accommodate groups of all sizes. The dining room seats 150, a patio and barbeque grill serves small groups, spacious booths seat 10, with room left over at the bar that encircles Sudwerk's brewkettle and mash tun. A bottling line is planned for an adjacent building.

Broward and Unger brought brewer Karl Elden from Germany. His brewing credentials are displayed in the bar where the fermentation tanks are visible behind a glass partition. From this point, customers can observe the creamy, meringue-like froth that forms during fermentation. It's a tantalizing sight to watch beer "working."

Sudwerk is along the I-80 corridor connecting the Bay with the Sacramento area that the *San Francisco Chronicle* says is destined for the state's greatest growth over the next decade. With Sudwerk in the middle of this corridor and near an interstate exit, it could become a regional brewery when its bottling line becomes operational. Sudwerk won a silver and bronze medal at the 1990 Great American Beer Festival.

Davis (pop. 40,000) is on the San Francisco-Sacramento-Lake Tahoe route where it is not unusual for people to drive an hour for dinner. This makes Davis' Back Alley and Sudwerk brewpubs ideally located as the suburban sprawl creeps toward Tahoe.

Brewpub menu: German-style foods, complete lunches and dinners

Hubsch Brau - light lager, with flowery hops, golden color
1990: 1200 barrels (opened in May)

TRUCKEE BREWERY/PIZZA JUNCTION
11401 Donner Pass Road
Truckee 95734   916-587-7411
President: Steve Downing
Brewer: Jean Luke
Equipment: Locally designed and manufactured

Truckee is a modest tourist town on the northern shore of Lake Tahoe where the altitude is more than 7,000 feet. Most of Truckee is located along Donner Pass Road where old hotels, saloons, and cafes look like a Western movie set. If a movie producer needed an old railroad for a scene, he could use Truckee's depot which still accommodates daily runs.

Truckee Brewery is the inspiration of Steve Downing, a former Lockheed aerospace engineer, and his wife, Peggy. The Downings worked with a friend, Gary Rausch, a refrigerator repairman, who added a brewery to their pizza restaurant. The Downings were helped by Steve's brother, Gene, who later started the Nevada City Brewery 45 miles away.

Steve Downing met Peter Coors, President of the Coors Brewery, at a Ducks Unlimited meeting in Reno a few years ago. Coors ran low on money while the two were gambling one night and Steve loaned Coors $200. Coors left early the next morning and forgot about the loan. Later, when he contacted Downing, he invited him to Golden. Coors offered technical assistance when Downing was building Truckee and a Coors techncian flew in when the brewery was under construction.

Peggy Downing has made Truckee Brewing/Pizza Junction into the most successful pizza operation in town. She sells 300 pizzas daily and makes dough fresh every morning. She grew up in an Italian household in San Francisco and recalled recipes from her childhood that she uses in the restaurant.

Brewpub menu: pizzas and pubfare

Light
Export Amber
Dark
1989: 250 barrels
1990: 300 barrels

BREWING IN THE GREAT NORTHWEST

MUNICH ON THE COLUMBIA,

THE WILLAMETTE , PUGET SOUND AND THE STRAIT OF JUAN DE FUCA

The Northwest corner of North America from the California border to the island archipelago off the coast of British Columbia is one of the continent's most abundant treasures of natural resources and scenic wonders.

The bounty of the Northwest is one of the richest in the world. Great schools of salmon swim upstream into rivers for spawning; neat orchards of apples, peaches, and cherries dot the valleys; bountiful vineyards on both sides of the Cascades produce superb wines; grains and vegetables grown in the irrigated farms along the Columbia River find their way to restaurant tables all over the world.

Unspoiled nature is another Northwest treasure. Climbers trek up snowy Mt. Rainer, Mt. Hood, Mt. Baker and other mountains along the Cascades. Kayakers and white water canoeists race down glacier-fed rivers. Campers and hikers trek through national and state parks to experience the serenity of the Northwest's mountains, meadows, and seashores. Sportsmen, adventurers, and pioneers searching for an exciting lifestyle can have their fantasies fulfilled in this rugged but romantic land.

Culture in all forms also flourishes in Seattle, Portland, Vancouver, Victoria and the numerous college and university towns throughout the Northwest. Seattle's Art Museum, Seattle Center, Seattle Repertory, Victoria's British Columbia Provincial Museum, Maritime Museum of British Columbia, Portland's Center for the Performing Arts, the Portland Art Museum, and the Oregon Historical Center are all superb examples of the dedication to regional culture.

Because of these riches, the Pacific Northwest has attracted millions of new residents from Canada, the U.S., and all over the world who desire an active lifestyle in a beautiful setting. The Northwest truly has it all: snow-capped mountains, rocky coastlines, quaint seaports, emerald forests, white water rivers, and abundant locally grown or harvested foods -- salmon, oysters, apples, cherries, blackberries, grapes, and grain.

CASCADIA: A SHARED CULTURE

The common interests shared by Oregon, Washington, and British Columbia has led in recent years to discussions that the two states and one province have powerful reasons to consider themselves as one entity rather than three political jurdictions divided by an international border. Proponents describe the region as "Cascadia" with common economic, cultural, environmental, educational and political objectives.

The idea that the Pacific Northwest has common historical interests is not new. At the beginning of the 19th century, the Oregon frontier extended as far north as British Columbia.

Cascadia presents an impressive portfolio of economic and political might: 529,000 square miles, more than 10 million people, three major ports forming a powerful trading consortium, and strong interest on the part of economic and social leaders to join forces into a regional power.

Business leaders in Vancouver and Seattle are discussing joint ventures to ease the transportation problems in moving goods and people across the border. A Seattle politician has proposed forming a consortium of universities in Cascadia to allow students from the region to attend any public university as residents. Leaders in the arts have proposed pooling resources to form an opera company shared by Seattle, Portland, and Vancouver. Legislators from five Northwest states (including Idaho, Montana, and Alaska) and two provinces (Alberta) have met to discuss pooling economic, energy, and environmental resources.

This vision of shared interests was described in the novel "Ectopia," published in 1975 by Ernest Callenbach that foresaw the region seceding in the 21st century to form a new nation known as an "ecological utopia." Clearly, the people of the Pacific Northwest are proud of their economic power, rich natural resources, and common language and culture. This pride extends to a belief that their destiny has been joined by forces that extend beyond political borders.

CRAFT BREWING AT ITS FINEST

It is little wonder then that the Northwest is also one of the most creative centers of craft brewing in North America. The excitement and dynamism that the people of the Northwest expect at work and at play they also demand in their food and drink. Northwest wineries are regarded as some of the finest in the world; salmon and crabs from Pacific waters off the Northwest coast are flown around the world daily.

And Northwest craft beers? They're also regarded as world class: hoppy English-style ales, hearty German-style lagers and wheat beers, smoky porters, Scottish ales, and spicy Belgian-style ales are all brewed locally by Northwest craft breweries. One publication called Portland "Munich on the Columbia" in tribute to the sophistication of the Northwest craft brewing industry.

The excitement of the craft brewing scene, however, is not restricted to excellent beers -- it also has much to do with the personalities of the brewers and what they have accomplished by making Northwest microbreweries an attraction for tourists and beer lovers alike. Touring Northwest craft breweries is the closest experience one can have to making a pilgrimage to Europe's classic breweries, attending Munich's Oktoberfest, or CAMRA's Great British Beer Festival. North America has its own heritage of classic breweries again. They shouldn't be missed.

PLANNING A NORTHWEST BREWPUB CRAWL

What makes the Northwest such an interesting place to visit is the diversity in craft breweries and the many fine beers they produce. Some three dozen microbreweries dot the Northwest landscape from scenic ski resorts in British Columbia to campus brewpubs in Washington and Oregon and charming fishing villages along the coast. Their diversity is not limited to the beer styles they brew but extends to the type of operation, setting, and atmosphere.

Northwest craft breweries that belong on a "must see" list include: Seattle's nouvelle Redhook Brewery, the tiny Pike Place Brewery, and Duwamps Cafe/Seattle Brewing; any of Portland's neighborhood brewpubs including a couple of the McMenamin's chain of 22 restaurants and brewpubs; the Yakima Brewpub in Yakima's old railroad depot; Victoria's Spinnakers and Swan's Brewpubs, Vancouver's Granville Island Brewery, and one of the microbreweries along Oregon's Willamette Valley. They're all worth the time to search out and experience their charm. All that is needed is a little time, a few directions, a thirst for good beer -- and a spirit of adventure.

THE TROLLEYMAN PUB AT THE BREWERY · TELEPHONE 206/548-8000 FOR INFORMATION

Seattle's Redhook Brewery and Trolleyman Pub. One of the Northwest's classic microbreweries. Noted for its distinctive ales, modern brewery, and comfortable pub.

A Northwest brewery adventure does not have to be focused on just traveling and tasting beer -- it can follow a white-water rafting trip, camping in a national park, fishing in a mountain stream, or treking along a remote seashore. Northwest beers always taste better after spirits are refreshed by clean air, vigorous exercise, and the restorative powers of the great outdoors

HEARTY, SPICY, COLORFUL ALES

One aspect that seems to unite Northwest craft breweries are their beers -- or ales to be precise. Most Northwest microbrewed beers are hearty, fruity, and complex top-fermented ales that might not have as large a following in other geographic regions. But in the Northwest these distinctive ales match the charm of its people and their pride in their region.

Adding whole dried hops to the copper brewing kettle at Seattle's tiny Pike Place Brewery. Pike   Place has been called the Northwest's "microest micro."

Maybe it's the tangy salt-sea air, the refreshing piney woods, or the crisp mountain air -- whenever you're in the Northwest the only beer to drink is something that is fresh, robust, tasty, and as distinctive as the region itself.

It's no small matter that most Northwest beers are brewed from ingredients from nearby fields and farms: malted barley from Washington fields, hops from the sunny Yakima valley, and fresh water from the snowy Cascades Range. Northwest breweries take pride when they put on their advertising that their beers are locally brewed from locally grown crops.

NORTHWEST BEER PUBLICATIONS

A brewpub crawl would not be complete without catching up on the latest news from the craft brewery front. Three publications have started up in the Northwest to cover the latest news from the breweries. Pick up copies and follow the trend.

In Portland, the *Cascade Beer News* reports on Northwest microbreweries with plans to cover Alaska and California on a selected basis. The *Northwest Beer Journal* published in Seattle covers the brewing scene as well as restaurants and taverns that feature specialty beers. And the *Pint Post* published by the Seattle-based Microbrewery Appreciation Society (MAS) also features stories about microbreweries and brewing personalities.

All of the Northwest beer publications are mining the rich lore of beer, brewing events, beer tastings, and the colorful microbrewing personalities themselves. They're not only fun to read but also record the history of the Northwest craft brewing movement. One day beer historians and sociologists will pore over these publications to find out how this trend evolved.

NORTHWEST BEER FESTIVALS

Several beer festivals are held throughout the Northwest during the year. The largest in North America is the Oregon Beer Festival held in Portland the third week in July. The festival was first held in 1988 and sponsored by three Portland breweries: Widmer, Portland, and Bridgeport.

In 1990, the three-day event attracted 25,000 thirsty festival-goers who sampled 48 beers from as far away as Massachusetts, Minnesota, Colorado, and California. Portland's restaurants prepared special foods to go with the beers and local bands played throughout the afternoon. The combination of great beers, food, music, sunny weather, and efficient management has made the Oregon Brewers Festival the largest in the country.

Seattle holds a Northwest Ale Festival each June sponsored by the Microbrewery Appreciation Society. Numerous state and county sponsors also hold beer festivals throughout the year.

BRITISH COLUMBIA

British Columbia to Canadians is what California is to Americans. In terms of culture, lifestyle, and recreation, the province offers opportunities and resources not found in other parts of Canada. British Columbia's natural resources rival California's with wilderness areas, offshore islands, mountains, scenic rivers, and abundant parks.

Although British Columbia does not have California's large population, its demographics are similar. Waves of Asian immigrants have brought money, families, and customs to their new homeland as they have in California. A stroll down the streets of Vancouver will reveal Vietnamese, Chinese, Hong Kong, and Korean restaurants and shops similar to those found in San Francisco or Los Angeles.

British Columbia also resembles California by being a hothouse for trends, lifestyles, sports, and the arts. The province also is the birthplace for the entire North American brewpub movement. The first brewpub was started in Horseshoe Bay at the Troller Pub, a waterfront tavern a half-hour drive north of downtown Vancouver.

There could not have been a more scenic location for such an historic occasion. From the front window of the Troller Pub and the Horseshoe Bay Brewery a hundred yards away, customers can watch yachts, sailboats, and ferries dock in a wooded cove. Although the Troller and Horseshoe Bay Brewery are no longer united in their venture, the site is worth a visit to anyone interested in the history of microbrewing or the beauty of this tiny harbor.

VICTORIA

Victoria, on Vancouver Island, is British Columbia's capital, and about as close as one can get to a continental experience in North America. Vancouver Island is blessed not only with spectacular natural treasures in the mountains, rivers, rainforest, and abundant animal life, but also historical and cultural landmarks that rival other major cities in North America.

Most travelers arrive at the Queen City via the Inner Harbor ferries and are treated to a colorful display of gardens, flowing lawns, and flower baskets lining Government Street. The stately Empress Hotel at the Inner Harbor underwent a $45 million restoration in 1989 and is one of the city's landmarks. Whether spending a week or an afternoon in Victoria, travelers should plan on strolling through the Empress' lobby at 4 PM tea time and viewing the spectacular stained glass windows and attractive interior.

Greeting new arrivals at Victoria's Inner Harbor are vendors hawking guide services to tourist spots, wax museums, craft and souvenir shops. Along Government and Wharf Streets, horse-drawn carriages clip-clop in front of Queen Victoria's imposing statue on the lawn of the Parliament Building and the Royal British Columbia Museum. On the museum's rear lawn is Thunderbird Park with an impressive collection of totem poles crafted by the Inuit peoples. Victoria's other attractions include the Maritime Museum, Market Square, and Chinatown.

Victoria's history is rich with romantic tales of gold prospectors heading to Alaska, fishing fleets plowing the waters for salmon, and native Inuits who developed a rich culture long before the Hudson's Bay Company built a fort here in 1843 and named it after Queen Victoria. Pioneer homes have been preserved including the Lelmchen House, which dates back to 1852, and the Craigflower Manor, built in 1856.

Day-trippers over from Seattle or Vancouver can stroll down narrow streets and shop at boutiques, crafts shops, and galleries along Wharf Avenue and find bone china, handmade chocolates, and native crafts. Double decker buses accommodate those who have only a few hours and want to see the sights in the center of Victoria.

Victoria Visitors Information Centre: 604-382-2127

One should not restrict a visit to Vancouver Island to BC's capital city; the island's treasures spread the entire 280 miles from Victoria's Parliament Building on the southeastern tip to Cape Scott Park on the northwest coast. A few minutes out of Victoria, travelers on Saanich Peninsula discover farms, ports, quaint villages, and country inns. Special attractions a short distance from Victoria include Butchart Gardens, the Dominion Astrophysical Observatory, and the Forest Museum at Duncan.

Ferries sail to mainland destinations in Canada and the U.S. from Nanaimo, Courteney, and Port Hardy along Vancouver Island's eastern shore. These and other seaside villages and towns provide charter fishing boats and whale watching cruises through the Gulf Islands.

VICTORIA'S CRAFT BREWERIES

Four brewpubs and two microbreweries on Vancouver Island demonstrate a respectable presence of craft breweries to entice travelers to take a ferry for a visit. Victoria resembles England in more ways that just inns, double decker buses, and statues to Queen Victoria. The capital city's ales duplicate the originals brewed in native England.

Victoria Visitors Information Center: Inner Harbor, Government Street at Humboldt

Tourism Victoria: 6th floor, 612 View Street 604-382-2127

(to arrange accommodations, call 1-800-663-3883)

Munro Books: 1108 Government Street   604-382-2464

Royal British Columbia Museum: 604-387-3701

FOGG N' SUDS

A visit to British Columbia would not be complete without stopping by one of the Fogg n' Suds restaurants (four in Vancouver, one in Victoria). There are few restaurants that promote beer -- particularly craft brewed products -- better than this chain of pubs which features a neighborhood atmosphere where publicans greet patrons by name and know their favorite beers.

Fogg n' Suds' beverage menu (the cover photo displays 90 international beer bottles on a shelf) lists wines, cocktails, coolers, ciders, and more than 250 beers by region. A beer glossary helps customers develop an appreciation for the complexity of beer's color, appearance, aroma, and taste.

Fogg n' Suds has its own Passport Club which beer lovers can join for a nominal $2.50. They receive an authentic looking numbered passport whose inside pages contain entries for tasting 164 beers. After trying 40 beers, passport holders receive a free mug and passport photo that will be added to the pub's photo gallery.

As passport holders try more beers, they progress from the initial blue passport to silver, gold, platinum and diamond. Accordingly, they're promoted from Celebrator to Ambassador, Old Peculiar, Excelsior and eventually enter the Sovereign Hall of

Foam after tasting a staggering 400 different beers! Those august members receive a credit card, photo, diploma and 20% off food purchases for their devotion for answering the call.

Fogg n' Suds Vancouver:

Kitsilano - 604-732-3377

Broadway & Cambie - 604-872-3377

English Bay - 604-683-2337

Burnaby - (Lougheed Hwy & Bainbridge) 604-321-7837

Fogg n' Suds Victoria:

711 Broughton at Douglas - 604-383-2337

BRITISH COLUMBIA FERRY

Brewpub adventurers can experience a taste in ocean-going travel by taking a cruise on one of 38 BC ferrys which steam from Vancouver, Victoria, Seattle, and 39 other ports along the Northwest coastline. The impressive fleet of ferries feature snack bars, game rooms, card tables, broad decks, comfortable seating, and carpeting. It's a delightful break from the tedium of fighting traffic on overcrowded interstates while trying to enjoy the beauty of the Northwest.

Both Vancouver and Victoria can be reached from Seattle several times a day from Pier 48 at the downtown waterfront. Ferries also run regularly between Vancouver, Nanaimo, and Victoria. A private boating company operates two high-speed craft, the Victoria Clipper and Victoria Clipper II, for daily service between Seattle and Victoria. The trip takes 2 1/2-3 hours through the beautiful San Juan Islands separating the mainland and Vancouver Island (for reservations call 602-382-8100 in Victoria; 206-448-5000 in Seattle).

For travelers who have more than a few days to explore the British Columbia coast, a ferry travels from Port Hardy on the northern tip of Vancouver Island through the Inside Passage with stops at Bella Bella and Prince Rupert on the mainland and

Skidegate and Alliford Bay on the Queen Charlotte Islands. The Inside Passage route continues to Ketchikan, Juneau, and Haines, Alaska, a popular route during the summer.

BC Ferries:

Vancouver 604-669-1211

Victoria 604-386-3431

or write British Columbia Ferry Corporation

1112 Fort Street

Victoria V8V 4V2

Seattle 206-624-6663

BRITISH COLUMBIA

BUCKERFIELD'S BREWERY/SWAN'S RESTAURANT
508 Pandora Avenue
Victoria   V8W 1N6   604-361-3310
President: Michael Williams

Historic Victoria on the southern tip of Vancouver Island has the honor of being home to two of the most charming brew-pubs in North America. The Buckerfield Brewery, the more ambitious and decorative, is part of a bed & breakfast inn and restaurant facing Victoria's picturesque harbor. The area was once the heart of Victoria's old mercantile district.

Earlier in the century, the building was a grainary for Canadian wheat and barley destined for Far East ports. Swan's memorabilia include two giant wheels from an old elevator, rails from the old railroad, and the original laminated lumber in the pub ceiling.

Local entrepreneur Michael Williams, who purchased feed for his sheep-dogs in the granary when he was an immigrant, bought the building in 1988 and converted it into a brewpub inn. Williams named it The Swan for the Hans Christian Anderson fairy tale about the ugly duckling transformed into a beautiful swan.

Today, the Swan complex resembles an art gallery, sidewalk cafe, floral shop, and museum. Travelers can indulge by staying in one of the spacious 36 rooms in the inn, enjoy dinner or lunch outdoors or indoors, and have a fresh pint of Buckerfield's craft beers at the polished wooden bar. Swan's clientele are Victoria's sophisticated set who enjoy the colorful ambiance, the view of the harbor, and the excellent food and fresh beers.

Buckerfield Brewery was designed by Frank Appleton, a Canadian consult-ant who built the Troller Pub in Horseshoe Bay and Victoria's Spinnakers, the first two North America brewpubs. Buckerfield's beer is pulled from the basement brewery by traditional English beer engines.

Rates for Swan's B & B run from $85 in the winter to $110 during the peak summer season. A banquet room accommodates up to 95 people for conven-tions and meetings.

Brewpub menu: complete lunches and dinners; pubfare in the brewpub

Pandora Pale Ale - *brewed with crystal malt, Eroica and Cascade hops*
Buckerfield's Bitter - *British-style bitter, copper-colored*
Swan's Oatmeal Stout - *dark, heavy,*
Appleton Brown Ale - *named after brewer Frank Appleton; creamy brown, slightly sweet*

GRANVILLE ISLAND
1441 Cartwright Street
Vancouver   V6H 3R7   604-688-9927
President: Mitchell Taylor
Brewer: Jim Holden

Beneath the busy overpasses and high-ways near downtown Vancouver is the Granville Island area which was converted in the late 1960s from riverfront warehouses surrounded by mud flats into a bustling marketplace. Today, Granville Island's Public Market is a collection of fruit and vegetable stands, craft shops, bakeries, delis, and restaurants..

One of Granville Island's more interesting enterprises is a childrens' museum and toy store where weary parents can drop off the kids while visiting the market. Across from the children's store in a converted two-story warehouse is Canada's first "cottage brewery."

The eponymous microbrewery is the creation of two Vancouver entrepreneurs, Bill Harvey and Mitch Taylor, who also founded the city's False Creek Marina in the 1970s. They watched the early brewpubs open in Victoria and Horseshoe Bay and decided cosmopolitan Vancouver would support a local cottage brewery.

They raised $1.2 million and opened in June 1984. Six years later, Granville Island has sold more than 12 million bottles of Germany-style lagers and increased its original capacity from 5,000 hectoliters/year to 25,000 h/yr. Granville Island's beers are carried in 120 provincial liquor stores and 600 licensed accounts in British Columbia. Limited shipments have been made into the U.S., but their best market remains the British Columbia lower mainland.

In 1989, Granville Island was acquired by the International Potter Distilling Corporation, which also markets wines in Western Canada. The brewery's hospitality room sells clocks, glasses, mugs, hats, aprons, coasters, kegs, gift pacs, and wooden cases emblazoned with the brewery's logo. Daily tours start at 2:00 PM.

Island Lager - brewed with 2-row Canadian malt
Island Bock - brewed with three different malts; available in spring and fall
Island Light

1989: 12,000 hectoliters
1990: 15,000 hectoliters

HORSESHOE BAY BREWERY
6695 Nelson Avenue
West Vancouver   V7W 2B2   604-921-6116

President: David Bruce-Thomas
Brewmaster: Cameron Rolfe

- Brewers of Traditional Real Ale -

Horseshoe Bay is tucked into one of British Columbia's scenic harbors just a few miles north of downtown Vancouver. Every night, and particularly on weekends, hundreds of cars line up to take the BC ferry across to Sechelt Island to their homes or weekend retreats. In this small community nestled among the bay's woods, microbrewing pioneer John Mitchell began brewing small batches of ale in 1981.

British Columbia liquor board officials scratched their heads and had to come up with a ruling before the microbrewery could open. They decided that Mitchell could not sell direct to customers but had to have a separate outlet. A local pub, the Troller, agreed to carry Horseshoe Bay's ale and thus became the first North American brewpub even though its beer was made away from the restaurant.

John Mitchell moved on to open Spinnakers Brewpub in Victoria and David Bruce-Thomas, who started as the brewery's keg washer, became owner and brewmaster. After the Troller Pub closed, Horseshoe Bay continued brewing for two local outlets, Trolls Seafood Restaurant and Ya Ya's Oyster Bar, and later for the Two Parrots Pub in Port Coquitlam and the Rusty Gull in North Vancouver.

The brewery's front window looks out on Horseshoe Bay's harbor where ferries dock several times a day on their 30-minute journey across to the Sunshine Coast known for woodlands, trails, fishing villages, and hiking.

David Bruce-Thomas recently contracted with the Sunshine Coast Brewery across the bay in Sechelt. Horseshoe Bay will brew their beer which will be transported by ferry and bottled by Sunshine Coast.

ISLAND PACIFIC/VANCOUVER ISLAND BREWING
6809 Kirkpatrick Crescent, RR #3
Victoria   V8X 3X1   604-652-4722
President: Barry Fisher
Brewer: Ross Elliot

Vancouver Island Brewing is a division of Island Pacific which started operations in 1984. Island Pacific originally producing draught beer for restaurants, pubs, taverns, and home consumption in 50 and 20-liter containers.

Vancouver Island went through a reorganization and will be undergoing expansion in 1990 to produce six-packs of 12 oz. bottles.

Distribution will be limited to Vancouver Island and greater Vancouver.

Viking Lager - *German-style pilsener*
Key Lager - *Vienna-style amber lager*
Hermann's Dark Bavarian Lager - *Dortmunder-style lager*
Pipers - *a pale ale*

LEEWARD NEIGHBORHOOD PUB
649 Anderton Road
Comox   V9N 5B7   604-339-5400

Co-owners: Gilbert & Ronald Gaudry
Brewer: Robert H. Lamb
Equipment: Second-hand dairy equipment; tanks from Specific Mechanical Systems

Comox is a retirement and fishing village with a population of 3,500 on the east coast of Vancouver Island about an hour north of Victoria. Being on the water, the Leeward brewpub is decorated in a nautical theme with driftwood, diving gear, charts, seascape paintings, and sailing equipment.

The Gaudry father and son team built the Leeward Brewpub and opened in August 1984; theirs was the third brewpub licensed in Canada. They received the first Canadian license to bottle their beer for off-premise sale. The brewery uses malt extract to brew its four beers. When the beer is aged, it is pulled direct from holding tanks to the bar 340 feet away. Brewer Bob Lamb is a retired butcher who emigrated from England in 1977 and taught himself brewing.

Brewpub menu: complete dinners, specializing in seafood

Leeward lager
Leeward lite
Leeward pilsener
Leeward Dark British ale

OKANAGAN SPRING
2801 27A Avenue
Vernon   V1T 1T5   604-433-0088

President: Jakob Tobler
Brewer: Stefan Tobler

In 1985, two German immigrants, Jakob Tobler and Buko von Krosigk, opened a German-style brewery in Vernon east of Vancouver in the scenic Okanagan Valley famous for orchards and rich farmland.

Their first pint of Okanagan Spring Lager -- brewed according to the Reinheitsgebot Purity Law -- was poured on December 31, 1985. By the next fall, Okanagan's Old English Porter, Spring Lager, and Premium Lager were marketed to Vancouver. Two more beers were added in 1987: Old Munich Wheat Beer and St. Patrick Stout.

Okanagan has gone through two expansions in its brief history; it increased capacity in 1987 to 12,000 hectoliters and in 1988 to 25,000. Plans are underway to increase capacity to 60,000 hectoliters.

Old Munich Wheat - *brewed with 60% malted wheat, 40% 2-row barley malt, and top-fermented*

Olde English Porter - *after lagering, the wort is krausened for additional fermentation and bottle conditioned up to 3 months; 8.5% alcohol by volume; strongest beer brewed in Canada*

St. Patrick Stout - *brewed with 2-row black British and pale barley malts, medium heavy, unfiltered; 5.5% alcohol by volume*

Premium Lager - *Bavarian-style lager, brewed with 2-row malt; Hallertau hops, dry and hoppy; 5% alcohol by volume*

Extra Special Pale Ale - *copper-colored, British-style ale brewed with Northern Brewer hops; 5% alcohol by volume*

1989: 15,000 hectoliters
1990: 23,500 hectoliters

PRAIRIE INN COTTAGE BREWERY
7806 E. Saanich Road
Saanichton   V06 1M0   604-652-1575
President: Ted Anderson

Saanichton is a township north of Vancouver. The Prairie Inn brewpub opened in 1982. The brewery uses malt extract to produce its beers.

British Bulldog
Australian Rules Lager

SHAFTEBURY
1973 Pandora Street
Vancouver   V5L 5B2   604-255-4550
Co-owners: Timothy P.J. Wittig and Paul W. Beaton
Brewer: Paul W. Beaton
Equipment: Specific Mechanical Systems

Canadians love the term "cottage brewery," which is a homier expression than the American term "mom-and-pop" enterprise. To be honest, I prefer the

Canadian expression since it has a nostalgic flavor to it, as if these businesses started in a kitchen of a thatched cottage, moved into the basement, then the garage, and finally, if luck and good business fortune followed, might end up in a warehouse or industrial area.

Tim Wittig and Paul Beaton are known as cottage-brewers according to the British Columbia press that writes them up occasionally and marvels that a couple of "blokes" could actually brew a decent beer and make a business of it.

Wittig and Beaton, in fact, were college drinking buddies who started in 1986 to do something about beer other than just drink it. While students at the University of British Columbia, they fell in love with the idea of starting their own cottage brewery. They received a provincial small business loan and poured their first draught in August 1987.

Their plan was to produced British-style real ales even though neither Wittig nor Beaton had ever been to the British Isles. They built the brewery themselves on Pandora Street in Vancouver's East End with both of them doing drywalling, painting, and renovation. Start-up costs were a modest $200,000 Canadian, a sparse amount since brewing equipment alone can cost more than half that amount to get started. Beginning with a few accounts in the Lower Mainland, Shaftebury's sales have grown monthly. The brewery now has seven employees with annual sales totaling about $1 million. Shaftebury is Vancouver's only independently-owned brewery.

Shaftebury's beers are kegged real ales dispensed in nearly 100 establishments in Vancouver and Seattle. They can be identified by their familiar porcelain tap handles.

Shaftebury Bitter - light, hoppy amber ale
Shaftebury Cream Ale - nut-brown ale similar to a dark mild
Shaftebury E.S.B. - full-bodied copper ale
Christmas Ale (barley wine) - recipe includes molasses and sugar cane syrup which has a staggering 9.2% alcohol by volume

1989: 4,000 hectoliters
1990: 7,000 hectoliters

SPINNAKERS BREWPUB
308 Catherine Street
Victoria V9A 3S8 604-384-6613
President: Paul Hadfield
Brewers: Jake Thomas, Brad McQuay

One of Victoria's most beautiful settings is the Inner Harbor where sailboats, ferries, and yachts sail every day. Just a few yards from the waterfront is Spinnakers, Canada's first brewpub, which is situated so that everyone in the pub can watch ships sail in and out of the harbor. Across from Spinnakers is the British Columbia's Parliament building and the skyline of the Queen City.

Paul Hadfield, one of Spinnakers' founders, is a former architect who used his international experience to design a modern building that combines aesthetics, efficiency, hominess, and charm. The casual atmosphere has much to do with the success Spinnakers has had in attracting a following throughout the Northwest. Whenever people in the Northwest talk about brewpubs, Spinnakers is one of the first to be recommended.

Part of Spinnakers' success are its spendid ales. Many are cask-conditioned and all are dispensed via piston-driven beer engines topped with porcelain tap handles. Spinnakers ales are served at the cellar temperature of 53 F.

Brewer Brad McQuay delights in brewing special ales such as Dunkel Krieken Weizen Brau, a blend of Belgian-style cherry beer with a full-bodied wheat beer! You aren't likely to find this style showing up soon at your local liquor store, but if you're within a thousand miles of Victoria, it might be worth a side trip to see what all the excitement is about.

The most popular item on Spinnakers' menu is fish and chips made with brewers yeast. Breads are baked with spent grains, yeast, and wort; the result is malty, dark breads with crisp crusts and thick texture. Delicious!

Spinnakers has had its share of difficulties with British Columbia provincial liquor authorities who place seating limits on restaurants and pubs. Spinnakers' original license permitted only 65 seats in the brewpub and the owners have been struggling to raise the number so they can open an outdoor patio and upstairs dining room. Spinnakers spawned two brewpubs in Seattle called Noggins -- one in the downtown Westlake Shopping Center and a second at the University of Washington campus. The second Noggins closed in 1990. The campus brewpub was in a renovated church with high ceilings, wooden floors, and an upstairs mezzanine.

Brewpub menu: chowders, salads, burgers, and special items including Oysters Rockefeller, Angels on Horseback (oysters wrapped in bacon and baked), mountain-high apple pie

Spinnaker Ale - amber, hoppy, light bodied
Mitchell's ESB - copper-colored, complex with malty fruitiness
Highland Scottish Ale - dark, sweet, malty ale in Scottish tradition
Mt. Tolmie Dark Ale - dark red, sweet, brewed with British pale malt and Scottish amber malt; less hoppy than English ales
Empress Stout - malty, dry, and creamy

SUNSHINE COAST
P.O. Box 1533
Sechelt   V0N 3A0   604-885-7074
President/Brewer: Lynn Rickveil

Sunshine Coast Brewery, on British Columbia's rocky west coast north of Vancouver, was started five years ago. In late 1990, Lynn Rickveil, a pulp mill worker from nearby Gibson who had worked in the brewery, took over ownership and struck an agreement with the Horseshoe Bay Brewery across the water.

Under the agreement, Horsehoe Bay will brew beer and Sunshine Coast will finish, bottle, and ship to accounts on British Columbia's Lower Mainland. Sunshine Coast's ales are brewed with English 2-row barley, British Columbian and German hops. Contract brewing for other microbreweries is in the plans for Sunshine Coast.

Peninsula Spring Ale - English-style bitter
Orca Lager - British malt extract brew

WHISTLER BREWING
1209 Alpha Lake Road
Whistler   V0N 1B0   604-932-6185

President: Rob Mingay
Brewer: Doug Nicholson
Equipment: Used European brewkettle, Ripley tanks

The village of Whistler is nestled in the mountains about two hours north of Vancouver and is a popular resort for British Columbia sportsmen and tourists.

Rob Mingay and Gerry Hieter raised $1.25 million to open their microbrewery on October 7, 1989 in an industrial park eight km. south of Whistler. They hired veteran German brewers, Herman Hoeterer and Bart Traubeck, who have been involved with start-up Canadian microbreweries, to come up with recipes for their beers. Within a year Whistler established itself locally and with Vancouver restaurants, pubs, and liquor stores. According to Hieter, 75% of Whistler's beers are sold five minutes from the brewery.

A financial windfall for the brewery has been contract brewing for area restaurants. Whistler brews a pale ale called Albino Rhino for the Earl's chain of 14 restaurants in British Columbia. It is a blend of pale Saskatchewan and British Carastan malts, Yakima's Cascade, and Oregon's Willamette hops; it resembles an English bitter with a long, clean finish. Whistler also produces a house brand ale for the Chateau Whistler Resort.

Whistler plans to expand their 17,400 sq.ft. brewery in 1991 to take advantage of their success and export to Washington state. Tours are scheduled on Saturday and Sunday, 1:00 & 2:30 PM.

Whistler Premium Lager - *full-bodied German lager, mild, hoppy*
Whistler Black Tusk Ale - *a blend of British black malt and 2-row Canadian barley yields a "dark" light ale*

1989: 6,500 hectoliters
1990: N/A

WASHINGTON

Washington state boasts one of the most pleasant and healthful lifestyles in the country. National and state parks, rocky coastlines, and abundant forests offer recreational activities that could keep a family busy for an entire vacation. A combination of cultural activities, a mixed economy, proximity to Asian markets, a bustling seaport and a diverse population make the state as rich in opportunities as it is in natural resources.

One of Washington's major attractions is the abundance of natural wonders. Foremost among these are the Cascades Range and its spectacular chain of a nearly extinct volcanic ridge formed by Mt. Rainier (14,410 ft.), Mt. Hood, Mt. St. Helens (8,365 ft.), and Mt. Baker (10,778 ft.). Even in summertime, the snowy mountain peaks are visible from 100 miles away.

The Cascades dominate the western quarter of the state from the Columbia River in the south to the Canadian border at the 49th parallel. From the south to the north runs a nearly continuous chain of national parks, forests, and wilderness areas that offer facilities for hikers, campers, climbers, and naturalists.

Another of Washington's natural wonders is the Olympic peninsula across Puget Sound from Seattle. The Olympic National Park dominates the peninsula with rainforests, streams, and mountain peaks including Mt. Olympus (7,965 ft.) and Mt. Carrie (6,995 ft.). Port Angeles on the north coast is a jumping off point to Vancouver Island. At this northernmost point on Highway 101, ferries sail daily across the Strait of Juan de Fuca to Victoria.

WASHINGTON'S MICROBREWERIES

Washington is also rich in the tradition of craft brewing. The state boasts a dozen microbreweries and brewpubs with the majority clustered in the Seattle area. Although many consider Seattle the heart of Washington's craft breweries, operations are scattered throughout the state from the Olympic peninsula to the wheat farming western half of the state. The towns of Kalama, Yakima, Poulsbo and Colville may not be as well-known as Seattle, but they are the homes of microbreweries that rank with the finest on the West Coast. Serious beer travelers should not consider a trip to Washington complete without visiting these distant but distinguished microbreweries.

SEATTLE

Seattle, the 25th largest city in the nation, resembles San Francisco with its hilly terrain, international center of commerce, comfortable lifestyle, and scenic waterfront. San Francisco has Fishermans' Wharf crammed with souvenir shops and restaurants; Seattle has Pike Place Market where vendors sell vegetables, fruits, fish, and crafts from stalls on Puget Sound.

Pike Place Market is the oldest surviving farmers market in the country and is listed in the National Register of Historic Places. Every day thousands of tourists and city residents stop by to purchase fresh fish, specialty foods, and produce. On weekends local artisans sell their wares from booths and stalls.

Not far from Pike Place Market is Pioneer Square in Seattle's historic district (also listed in the National Register of Historic Places) where the city's first settlement started in 1852. The site was occupied by the Duwamish Indians whose Chief Sealth was the namesake of the city. Today, Pioneer Square is crowded with restaurants, taverns, shops, art galleries, bookstores, and the Kingdome where the Mariners and Seahawks do battle against National League and NFL opponents. Two blocks from the Kingdome is the Pacific Northwest Brewpub that dispenses English- style ales.

A popular activity for Seattle tourists is the Underground Tour of Pioneer Square's hidden passageways that survived the Seattle Fire of 1889. Along the waterfront, tourists can take harbor cruises through Puget Sound or ferries to the Olympic peninsula or Vancouver Island.

A 10-minute walk from Pioneer Square is Seattle's International District with Asian markets and shops and Westlake Center, the newest downtown shopping arcade. A monorail from Westlake still runs to the site of the 1962 World's Fair and the towering Space Needle with its rotating rooftop restaurant.

THE HEART OF NORTHWEST CRAFT BREWING

Seattle is a garden of delights for the beer traveler. Not only are there microbreweries and brewpubs to visit but scores of restaurants and taverns that dispense fresh beer that rivals any other region in the world. Spicy ales, robust lagers, and smoky stouts can be found throughout the Puget Sound corridor that stretches from the Canadian border to the Columbia River.

A Seattle brewpub crawl is an excellent introduction to the variety of microbrewing enterprises. Such a venture could begin with a visit to the ultra-modern Redhook Brewery in the Fremont neighborhood, followed by a 10-minute drive to the University of Washington campus for a beer at the Big Time Brewpub, then downtown for lunch at the Pacific Northwest Brewpub in the Pioneer Square and a stroll up Western Avenue to the Pike Place Brewery. After a busy day of brewpub crawling, the fitting end of the day means dinner at the bistro-like Duwamps Cafe, home of Seattle Brewing, with its European-style menu and view of Puget Sound from the second floor lounge.

RESTAURANTS, PUBS, AND TAVERNS

Seattle boasts more than just innovative microbreweries and brewpubs. Food and drink are specialties of the Northwest and

Seattle's restaurants have few rivals when it comes to celebrating fine food and the Northwest's finest beers. Notable are Murphy's Pub and Cooper's Northwest Ale house not far from the University of Washington campus. Murphy's is an Irish Pub while Cooper's serves only West Coast microbreweries from 22 taps. Cooper's has house brands brewed by Hale's Ales called Cooper's Own and Old Mashie #3 and hosts the week-long Northwest Ale Festival each summer.

The Horse Brass Pub on SE Elmont, La Boheme on Phinney Avenue, and Latona by Greenlake pride themselves on their Northwest ales. Taverns outside Seattle that feature specialty beers are the Engine House #9 in Tacoma, the Heron and Beaver Pub in Seaview, and Cromwell's Ale House in Gig Harbor.

A Seattle tavern chain started by Mike McHugh has been a leader in promoting Northwestern craft beers and beer dinners. McHugh's restaurants include the Leschi Cafe, New Jake O'Shaughnessey's in Bellevue, Roasters in Kirkland, Issaquah Roost and downtown Vic & Mich's. The showpiece McHugh restaurant is F.X. McRory's in the shadow of the Kingdome. The 19th century-style saloon boasts 26 beers on tap amidst memorabilia, paintings, lithographs, and Old Seattle artifacts. It's a modern saloon thats shows how specialty beers, Northwest foods, art, and architecture can produce a classic effect.

Several Seattle-area taverns carry cask-conditioned ales -- naturally carbonated, non-filtered beer dispensed via old-style beer engines or gravity pulls. Cask-conditioned ales imitate the classic style made famous by England's CAMRA Real Ale movement. Consider cask-conditioned real ale one of the most pampered beers you'll ever try -- and try them you should. Find out why CAMRA revolutionized the British brewing industry when it started the real ale movement 30 years ago which lead to the North American microbrewing revolution.

NORTHWEST BREWPUB TOURS

A touring company in Seattle helps tourists make the rounds of local microbreweries and taverns. Northwest Brewery and Pub Tours offers afternoon or evening tours of 3 1/2 hours which includes transportation, beer samples, snacks, and souvenirs for $22 per person (206-547-1186).

BC Stena Line at Pier 48: 206-624-6986

Boeing Tours: 206-342-4801

Underground Tours: 206-682-4646

Washington State Ferries: 206-448-5000

Elliott Bay Book Company (Pioneer Square): 206-624-6600

WASHINGTON

BIG TIME BREWERY & ALEHOUSE
4133 University Way NE
Seattle 98105   206-545-4509

President: Reid Martin
Brewer: Ed Tringali
Equipment: JV Northwest

Big Time is the second brewery started by Reid Martin; his first, which he opened with his brother in 1986, is Triple Rock Brewery near the UC-Berkeley campus. The Berkeley brewpub was so successful that Reid took the concept north and opened Big Time near the Seattle campus of the University of Washington in December 1988.

The 125-seat Big Time brewpub is a copy of the Berkeley brewpub. Big Time's neighbors are the usual campus quik-copy shops, pizza joints, T-shirt shops, coffee houses, bookstores, and ethnic restaurants.

Big Time's menu of sandwiches, soups, chips, and salads is designed to meet the demands of Husky students. In addition to regular beers, Big Time brews seasonal ales including Centennial Rye Ale, Uncle Bison's Dunkel Weizen, and Oktoberfest Alt -- all reportedly made with a full pint of malted barley per pint of ale! Big Time's beers are unfiltered and unpasteurized and have an alcoholic content between 3.5%-4.5% by volume. The 14-barrel brewhouse was built by JV Northwest, who also supplied the Berkeley brewpub.

Prime Time Pale Ale
Atlas Amber Ale
Coal Creek Porter

1989: 200 barrels
1990: 1,116 barrels

FORT SPOKANE BREWERY
West 401 Spokane Falls Boulevard

Spokane 99205 509-838-3809

President: James Bockemuehl
Brewmaster: John Eyre
Equipment: JV Northwest brewkettle, mash lauter tun, fermentation tanks from old dairy equipment

The first brewpub to open in Spokane has a fascinating link to the history of brewing in America when the West was being settled. One hundred years ago Fort Spokane was a dusty frontier army fort when Washington was still a territory. Two brothers, Bernard and Max Bochemuehl, opened the original Fort Spokane Brewery in 1889 four miles south of Spokane where the Spokane and Columbia Rivers meet.

According to historical accounts, the brewery annually produced 2,000 barrels while the army fort was active. The brewery's loyal customers were army recruits, farmers, miners, loggers, trappers, and early settlers to eastern Washington.

The Bochemuehl brothers used a copper kettle to brew lagers from locally grown grains, wild hops and water from a nearby spring. During the summer, beer was kept cold by lowering it into a 100 feet deep, hand-dug cave behind the brewery. Today, the wild hops and man-made caves remain as legacies of the territory's first brewery.

The Fort Spokane microbrewery opened exactly a century after the original brewery opened in 1889. Its location in a reconverted bar near the mission area is across the street from the new convention center along the Spokane River front just a few miles from the original Bochemuehl brewery. President James Bochemuehl is a great-great nephew of the Bochemuehl brothers; he researched family records prior to reopening the brewery.

The microbrewery's early beers were brewed in food-grade plastic vessels; a 15-barrel brewhouse was added in 1990 with the first brew introduced on Valentines Day. The brewpub also sells plastic two-liter "to go" bottles that are dispensed from the cold box at the back of the brewery.

Brewpub menu: light dinners, salads, sandwiches, and pizza

Ben's Special Bitter *- dedicated to Ben Bockemuhel, owner of the original Fort Spokane brewery*

Pale Ale *- lighter ale made with all pale malt*

Pale *- an alt-style beer; light golden color*

Red Alt *- brewed with caramel and pale malts, Willamette hops and alt yeast*

Border Run Ale *- dedicated to Canadians who brewed beer and brought it across the border to thirsty Americans during Prohibition; brewed with Willamette and Yakima Tettnang hops*

Bulldog Stout *- heavy bodied with roasted barley flavor*

1989: 140 barrels
1990: 293 barrels

HALE'S ALES LIMITED (#2)
410 N. Washington
Colville   99114   206-827-4359
President: Mike Hale
Brewers: Phil O'Brien and Dave Metzger

Mike Hale is one of the pioneers of Northwest craft brewing. He spent 1981 on sabbatical as a brewer's apprentice at Gales Ales in Horndean, Hampshire, England. When he returned to America in 1982, he hand-built a 10-barrel brewery in Colville (5,000 population), 70 miles north of Spokane.

Mike Hale did all the welding, wiring, carpentry and brewing in the early years while his ales quietly developed a following, first in eastern Washington, then in western Washington, and finally throughout the Northwest. This was not an easy task since the area's beer drinkers were from predominantly conservative farming and foresting communities more used to fizzy pilseners than robust ales found in comfy English pubs.

Hale nostalgically recalls the fun, early days of microbrewing when he delivered beer in a 1946 fire truck (renamed the "Emergency Beer Delivery Unit"), staged impromptu Skakespeare on the brewery loading dock, and flew beer writer Michael Jackson over the Rocky Mountains to visit a Montana microbrewery (he even has a pilot's license).

After Hale's Ales had developed a regional market by the mid-1980s, Hale opened his second brewery in a Seattle suburb of Kirkland in 1987. The second Hale's brewery called mysteriously Hale's #1 makes the same ales as the original (now referred to as Hale's #2) but sells them in the thirsty Seattle and Northwest markets.

Pale American Ale - light, English-style bitter

Sheimo's Special Bitter - heavier bitter

Celebration Porter - dark, sweet porter honoring the original brewery's 100th batch of beer

Moss Bay Ales - light, malty, slightly sweet; known as MBA

Irish Ale - dark, lower alcohol ale

Wee Heavy - dark, heavier spiced seasonal ale that approaches 7% alcohol by volume

Harvest Ale

Cascade Mist

1989: 4,300 barrels (Hales #1 & #2)
1990: N/A

HALE'S ALES BREWERY (#1)
109 Central Way
Kirkland   99033   206-673-2962
President: Mike Hale
Brewers: Phil O'Brien and Dave Metzger

In 1987 Mike Hale opened his second brewery (called Hale's #1 even though it was the second) in Kirkland, a prosperous Seattle suburb, to satisfy the demand for his ales in Western Washington. Hale's #1 produces three times the volume of the original Colville brewery which supplies eastern Washington and Idaho markets.

Tourists strolling down Kirkland's Western Avenue smell the tangy aroma of ales brewing and can walk into Hale's for a quick tour. Hale's #1 is next door to a busy Roaster's Alehouse. Roaster's features neon signs, banners, trays, 150 tap handles, and T-shirts promoting specialty beers and microbreweries. Customers at Roaster's can choose from 18 specialty beers on tap and watch brewing going on next door through the windows at Hale's.

Lake Seattle is a short walk away and a visit to Hale's #1 allows one to view the splendor of Seattle's snow-capped mountains and waterways. Seattle's wet, cool weather is similar to England where ales are traditionally popular. All of Hale's #1 ales are kegged draft beer; Moss Bay Amber and Pale Ale are 65% of production. They also make house brand beers for Seattle restaurants and have 75 accounts in the city. Hale's advertising claims that customers prefer "a good pint of Hale's instead of the same old Rainier."

Pale American Ale

Sheimo's Special Bitter

Moss Bay Ales

Irish Ale

Wee Heavy

Harvest Ale

Cascade Mist

1989: 4,300 barrels (Hales # 1 & #2)
1990: N/A

HART BREWING
176 First Street
Kalama 98625 206-673-2962

President: Jack Bryce
Brewer: Clay Biberdorf
Equipment: Ripley's

The Hart brewery was started by a young couple, Tom Baune and Beth Hartwell, who left Seattle to move to Kalama and open their brewery in 1984. Tall, thin, tow-haired Baune could be a younger twin of British actor Peter O'Toole but dressed in a Pendleton shirt, jeans, and hiking boots.

The original Hart brewery was in a turn-of-the-century building that once served as Kalama's general store. Today, Kalama is divided by Interstate 5 linking Seattle and Portland. On the east side of I-5 is old Kalama; on the west side are logging mills, docks, and manufacturing plants. The new owners of Hart are moving the brewery across I-5 to the area along the Columbia River. The 8,000 square foot building was a part of the old Kalama Port Authority and will allow Hart to undergo a major expansion. Windows on three sides of the building will make for an attractive showcase, even if the brewery is in an industrial area.

Hart's unpasteurized ales are brewed with malted barley, wheat, and whole hops grown in the Pacific Northwest; the brewery's water is runoff from the glacial melt from Mount St. Helens, a few miles east of Kalama. With Hart's loyal following in the Northwest, the brewery could become a strong regional player when its new 30,000 barrel/year plant reaches capacity.

The ambiance for the original Hart brewery was chaotic warehouse with kegs, six pack and label cartons, malt and hop sacks stacked to the ceiling and an old counter where informal tastings were held. The mood of the original Hart Brewery seemed to say, "Hey guys, we're brewing in little Kalama next to the Columbia." The spacious, new facility makes a completely different statement: "Gentlemen, we've arrived and we're going Big Time!"

Pacific Crest Ale - *brewed with Willamette hops; a mild, slightly nutty ale*

Pyramid Pale Ale - *a well-hopped, English-style ale*

Pyramid Wheaten Ale - *the first draft wheat beer brewed in America since Prohibition*

Sphinx Stout - *hearty, black-as-coffee stout, well suited for damp, cold winter nights in the Northwest*

Snow Cap Ale - *a sweet, heavy, barley wine-style ale popular in the winter*

1989: 6,100 barrels

1990: 8,000 barrels

MARITIME PACIFIC BREWING
1514 NW Leary Way
Seattle 98107   206-782-6181
President: George Hancock
Brewer: Larry Rock

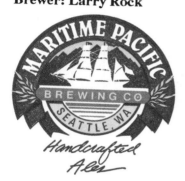

Maritime Pacific is the latest "micro-micro" to open in the Pacific Northwest. It is located in Seattle's Ballard maritime area on Leary Way where the Redhook Brewery got its start in 1984. Founder George Hancock is counting on the sophisticated palates of Northwest ale drinkers being attracted to his specialty German-style alt beers brewed with top-fermented yeast (alt is German for old).

Maritime Pacific's 17-barrel brewhouse is designed to produce 1,000 barrels/year, a considerable amount for a specialty brewery. In addition to its two main beers, Maritime Pacific eventually will produce a Dunkel-Weizen and Weizen seasonal beers.

Flagship Red Ale - *reddish, copper-colored altbier brewed with 20% wheat, pale, carastan, and Munich malts; Czech and Yakima hops*

Navigator Dark Ale - *dark, copper-colored Weizenbock brewed with 35% wheat; winter seasonal brew*

1990: 91 barrels (opened in November 1990)

NOGGINS WESTLAKE BREWPUB
400 Pine Street
Seattle   98101   206-682-2739

President: Paul Hadfield
Equipment: Specific Mechanical Systems

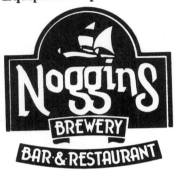

Noggins Westlake is one of two brew-pubs developed by the group that started Spinnakers Brewpub in Victoria, BC in the mid-1980s. Noggins Westlake is in a downtown Seattle retail area near Nordstroms and other outlets. Noggins is on the second floor of a two-story food court alongside pizza and pasta shops, delis, and cafes that cater to lunchtime shoppers.

Noggins Westlake started slowly, no doubt suffering from the sparse nightime traffic when brewpubs are busiest. A bottling line is planned to retail specialty ales.

A second Noggins opened in 1989 near the University of Washington campus. Noggins #2 was located in a church, but even after architectural redesign created a warm, open-air atmosphere, it closed in 1990. One observor commented wryly: "If God couldn't bring people into the building, how could a brewpub?"

Brewpub menu: pubfare, fish and chips

Noggins Ale - hoppy, golden-colored

Taylor's Special Bitter (SOB) - fruity, English-style bitter with mild, hoppy aroma

McQuay's Scottish Ale - dark, amber-colored ale with sweet, malty flavor from British pale and Scottish amber malts

Westlake Dark Ale - reddish-colored, coffee-like taste

Fitzpatrick Stout - malty, dry, but creamy stout

1989: 614 barrels
1990: 600 barrels

PACIFIC NORTHWEST
322 Occidental Avenue South
Seattle   98104   206-621-7002
President: Richard Wrigley

Pacific Northwest opened in September 1989 in historic Pioneer Square near the Seattle Kingdome. The neighborhood has boutiques, cafes, used book stores, and curio shops. The brewpub was the third by Englishman Richard Wrigley who started New York's first brewpub, Manhattan Brewing, and Boston's Commonwealth Brewery.

Pacific Northwest is similar in appearance to Wrigley's East Coast predecessors: shiny copper vessels, high-ceilings, and open areas for crowds. The horseshoe-shaped bar, red-brick interior, rows of wooden-jacketed storage tanks, and spaciousness creates the feeling of being in a working brewery. Pacific Northwest is one of the largest brewpubs on the West Coast. The 5,500-sq. ft. main floor brewery/restaurant seats over 200; the downstairs storage area destined to become a jazz club is 4,500-sq. ft.

Pacific Northwest's beers are English-style ales, porters, and stouts brewed with a combination of European and Canadian malts and European and American hops. English beer engines draw beer from the basement to the horseshoe-shaped bar. After the publican has drawn a pint, it takes a full minute for the creamy head to subside. It's a tantalizing process to watch while your tastebuds are being stimulated.

Wrigley left school when he was 16 and traveled for years before getting into the restaurant business. His ambition is to return to England in a few years and run for the European Parliament.

Brewpub menu: lunches and dinners featuring seafood, appetizers, sandwiches and salads

Blond Ale - light, dry ale with aromatic Saaz hops
Gold Ale - hoppy, golden-colored ale
Bitter - bronze-colored, authentic English bitter
Amber - mellow, full-bodied amber ale, slightly sweet
Stout - malty, roasted flavor
Porter - creamy, well-balanced

1989: N/A
1990: N/A

PIKE PLACE BREWERY
1432 Western Avenue
Seattle 98101 206-622-1880

President: Charles Finkel
Brewer: John Farias
Equipment: Customed designed by Vince Cottone

Charlie Finkel finally has his own brewery. After spending more than a decade as the founder and marketing wizard behind Merchant du Vin, a specialty beer importing company headquartered in Seattle, he was finally able to build his own brewery at home.

Pike Place was called, "the microest micro" when it opened in October 1989 with a parade to Cutters Bayhouse, a restaurant in the Pike Place Market. The tiny brewery shares space with the Liberty Malt Shop, Seattle's oldest homebrew shop, which opened in 1921 and was kept busy during Prohibition.

The brewery/homebrew shop are squeezed into a narrow storefront along Western Avenue. The copper brewkettle can be seen through the front window and makes an inviting scene. Beer magazines, books, and homebrew equipment are sold in the cramped homebrew shop at the front. Brief tours and tastings are conducted during the day.

Small is definitely beautiful in the case of Pike Place and what it may lack in size, it makes up in charm and ambiance. A tour takes only 10 minutes but it would be the rare traveler who would want to spend less than an hour talking to the help and sampling the delightful beers.

The technical design for the brewery was the work of Vince Cottone, a Seattle beer writer and consultant who has been active in the Northwest microbrewing field. Designer bottles of Pike Places beers are sold at the brewery. Even though bottles are returnable, most people keep them because of their classic design.

Pike Place Pale Ale - a refreshing, authentic English-style ale with abundant hops and malty taste
Pile Place Stout - a delicious, creamy stout with a pleasant nutty aftertaste that lingers

1990: 1,300 barrels

REDHOOK BREWERY
3400 Phinney Avenue North
Seattle   98103   206-548-8000

President: Paul Shipman
Brewer: Al Triplett
Equipment: Anton Steinecker Mashinenfabrik GmbH, Germany

Paul Shipman and Gordon Bowker founded Seattle's Redhook Brewery in 1981 and brewed their first beer in August 1982. Shipman was in the wine business with the Chateau Ste. Michelle and Bowker had started entrepreneurial ventures including the popular Starbucks coffees.

Redhook expanded in 1988 and moved from the maritime Ballard area to the Fremont neighborhood 10 minutes from the University of Washington. Redhook's new brewing equipment came from the Anton Steinecker Maschinenfabrik in Freising, Germany. The computer-operated, state-of-the-art equipment allows brewers to transfer batches from vessel to vessel without manual work.

The new location in a converted Trolley Barn allowed Redhook to build the Trolleyman Pub for customers to sample Redhook's ales fresh at the brewery. The Trolleyman's homey atmosphere attracts friends, neighbors, students, and beer tourists who stop by for a cup of Starbuck's coffee in the morning and a fresh Redhook in the afternoon.

Redhook's ales have received popular support throughout the Northwest and have won numerous brewing awards. Redhook's success is similar to that of San Francisco's Anchor Brewery. Both produce distinctive, high-quality beers and employ sophisticated marketing to develop a passionate following. Redhook is the model by which other Northwest microbreweries are compared; in a few years the well-managed, resourceful brewery could become a major regional brewery. Redhook's first major marketing outside the Northwest was its move in 1990 into northern California where specialty beers are well-established in the marketplace.

Redhook Ale - brewed with 2-row Klages, caramel, and black malt; Clusters, Willamette, Eroica, Cascades, Yakima, and Hallertau hops; a nutty, spicy ale similar to Belgian lambic ale

Redhook ESB - a rich, highly-hopped ale with a crisp finish

Ballard Bitter - chocolatey, malty flavor with distinctive, hoppy aroma

Blackhook Porter - coffee-colored, highly-hopped

Winterhook Christmas Ale - brewed with English pale, crystal malt, and malted wheat; golden brown, complex, rich tasting

Wheat Hook Wheaten Ale - mild, refreshing, crisp tasting

1989: 15,496 barrels
1990: 23,000 barrels

ROSLYN BREWING
33 Pennsylvania Avenue
Roslyn   98941   509-649-2232

Co-owners: Roger Beardsley and Dino Enrico
Brewer: Dino Enrico
Equipment: Combination of recycled dairy tanks and locally manufactured materials

Roslyn is one of several West Coast microbreweries located in off-the-interstate, over-the-mountain-pass, along-the-country-road places that makes a drive to visit them a treat.

Roslyn is 1 1/2 hours over Snoqualmie Pass in the Cascades Range east of Seattle along I-90. Roslyn's rustic mountain setting is so authentic that ABC-TV producers shoot background footage here for the "Northern Exposure" program that takes place in an Alaskan village in the mid-1950s. TV crews converted the town's wooden museum into an old-fashioned barber shop and coaxed a moose to stroll down main street for a shooting. The town still looks much like it must have 40 years ago before ski resorts and condos started popping up east of the Cascades.

Volunteers in Roslyn's museum boast that around the turn of the century, immigrants from 22 nations worked in coal mines, entertained themselves in Roslyn's 24 saloons, and ended their days in the 26 cemeteries that still dot the hillsides. A ledger book in the museum records business transactions of the original Roslyn Brewery that started in 1889. Saloons which carried Roslyn beer include the San Francisco, the Brick (which still operates), Terrino, and the Bon Ton.

The new Roslyn microbrewery is the joint effort of Roger Beardsley and Dino Enrico, whose ancestors grew up in the area. The two partners were burned out on the fast-paced life west of the Cascades and wanted to begin a new life more to their liking. Their first keg went out the door on May 18, 1990 to the Brick tavern, Washington's oldest tavern, and an early customer of the original brewery.

Roslyn's main street brewery facade resembles a modern Western saloon; a proposed taproom and hospitality area will draw beer tourists searching for an authentic old West locale along the brewpub trail. Roslyn is only making one beer at the present time and the brewery's modest production is limited to a few local accounts in town and the neighboring community of Cle Elum. Eventual plans should see Roslyn move westward across Snoqualmie Pass into the Seattle market.

Roslyn Beer - *although the brewers prefer to call their sole product only "beer," its style is closest to a mellow porter; clean, refreshing, and mildly sweet*
1990: 140 barrels (began brewing May 1990)

SEATTLE BREWING/DUWAMPS CAFE
301 Queen Ann Avenue North
Seatte 98109 206-281-8200
President: Phil Rogers
Brewer: Dick Cantwell
Equipment: JV Northwest

Phil Rogers sold his handsome Napa Valley brewpub, the Calistoga Inn, in 1989 and immediately he and his wife, Susan Benz, began looking for another location to build another brewpub. The Rogers eventually decided on Seattle because of the attractive Northwest style of life, the numerous recreational opportunities, and the beer consciousness of the area. The Rogers chose the Queen Ann neighborhood which resembles San Francisco's Telegraph Hill or Washington's Georgetown areas. They renovated a building that had been a restaurant since 1976 and opened for business in September.

The 250-seat Duwamps Cafe resembles a European bistro with a sidewalk cafe, restaurant on two levels, light, warm colors, and a casual ambiance. It is located a few blocks from downtown near the Opera House, Coliseum, and Space Needle. A second floor lounge overlooks Puget Sound.

Duwamps began brewing in November 1990 and expects to have three beers available at all times along with one seasonal beer.

Red Ale
Pale Ale
Dark Lager
1990: N/A (began brewing November 1990)

THOMAS KEMPER BREWING
22381 Foss Road N.E.
Poulsbo   98370   206-697-1446
Co-owners: Will Kemper and Andy Thomas
Brewer: Randy Reed

Thomas Kemper Brewery is the eponymous creation of its two founders, Will Kemper and Andrew Thomas. They opened their brewery in 1984 on Bainbridge Island across Puget Sound from Seattle. Thomas had been a Seattle engineer and Kemper a chemical engineer when they decided to change careers to become full-time brewers.

The original Kemper Brewery was moved in 1986 into the old family-owned Foss meat packing plant outside Poulsbo, a few miles west in a wooded area. Poulsbo resembles a charming Norwegian fishing village tucked into fjord-like waterways and surrounded by forests and the towering Olympic Mountains. The town was settled by Norwegian immigrants and landmarks from those days include St. Olaf Church and Fjord Drive. An annual Viking Fest honors Poulsbo's Scandinavian heritage.

The modest Kemper Brewery has a quaint, rustic taproom where lunches are served and a beer garden that accommodates parties. Hanging flowerpots and gardens are an invitation to enjoy beer in a wooded setting like one might find in Scandinavia.

The most fitting description of Thomas Kemper is that it is what you'd expect of a Norwegian brewpub. You'd walk in and see a room full of blonde, rosy-cheeked hikers quaffing beers, singing folk songs, and looking as if life would never be finer than it is at that time and place.

Thomas Kemper is only an hour and a half east of Seattle by ferry and a short drive from Winslow, but it is more a step back in time, place, and mood. From bustling and noisy Seattle, one crosses Puget Sound and is seduced by the scenic woods, crisp piney air, and mountain serenity. It makes the journey a mission of joy and wonder. Don't miss it.

Kemper's authentic German-style lagers are stored in cold fermentation tanks for a month at 33 F to produce a mellow, smooth finish. They are cold filtered but not pasteurized. Kemper's original Helles lager developed a distinctive blueberry flavor that enjoyed a dubious following for a time. The yeast was altered in the laboratory to eliminate the fruitiness. The pilsener and Dunkel recipes were also reformulated to produce greater balance.

Helles - *European pilsener, creamy head, with a crisp dry finish*

Dunkel - *dark, mahogany color, creamy head, hoppy and mellow; nice dry finish*

Pilsener

Oktoberfest

Winterbrau

1989: 2,500 barrels
1990: 3,000 barrels

YAKIMA BREWING & MALTING
25 North Front Street
Yakima   98901   509-457-6782
President: Bert Grant
Brewers: Dan Boutillier & Darren Waytuck
Equipment: Designed by Bert Grant; locally manufactured

Bert Grant is the Godfather of the North American microbrewing movement. He claims the distinction of opening the first brewpub in America since Prohibition in July 1982 in Yakima, a town internationally famous for its cherry, peach, and apple orchards and hop farms. Grant's first beer, which has become legendary, was Scottish Ale.

Grant was born in Scotland in 1928 and began working in Toronto during World War II as a brewing chemist. He worked for years as a brewing consultant and is considered one of the leading lecturers on brewing science. He has authored numerous articles, a basic text on brewing, and attends brewing conferences and seminars around the world.

In 1983, Grant started his Yakima brewpub in the old Opera House and immediately developed a following in the emerging field of craft brewing. Many early microbrewers traveled to Yakima to visit Grant's landmark brewpub. Today, as they were years ago, Grant's superb ales are spoken of with a reverence as some of the finest beers in the Northwest.

In February 1990, Yakima Brewing moved across the street to the turn-of-the-century railroad depot which is five times larger than the Opera House. The new brewpub includes a fireplace, brass railings, and a glassed-in garden room for enjoying Yakima's sunny weather. The homey brewpub resembles a Scottish pub complete with dartboards, newspaper stand, pub towels, Scottish plaids, and railroad memorabilia.

Grant's Scottish Ale - strong, hoppy with character and balance; very fine

Grant's Imperial Stout - dark, rich, and strong in the tradition of the 19th century Russian Imperial Stout served to the Romanov tsars; high alcohol content, excellent dessert or sipping beer

Grant's India Pale Ale - hoppy, aromatic English-style bitter

Grant's Celtic Ale - lighter beer, 100 calories per bottle, flavorful

Grant's Wheat Beer - wheat malt is added with pale malt to produce refreshing summer time beer best served with lemon or lime wedge

Grant's Yakima Cider - traditional hard cider made with pure apple juice and yeast; about 6% alcohol

Grant's Spiced Ale - Winter warmer with ginger, nutmeg, and other spices; a traditional holiday drink that can be heated to create 19th century mulled ale popular in Victorian times

1989: 4,261 barrels
1990: 4,558 barrels

OREGON

Driving down Interstate 5 along the Willamette River Valley, the traveler is lured to pull off the road and head into one of Oregon's small towns, valleys, or forests to indulge in the state's extraordinary beauty. Outdoor recreation is one of Oregon's greatest treasures: winter skiing, summer hiking in wilderness areas, fishing in fresh-water streams, and clam digging in chilly tidal waters. Another Oregon resource are the university campuses of Eugene, Salem, and Corvallis, and colorful towns like Bend, Ashland, and Newport.

Oregon prides itself on its microbrewing heritage. Not only was it home to one of the first microbreweries, Cartwright Brewing, but it also represents one of the most creative centers for North American craft brewing. The state's brewing heritage includes nearly two dozen microbreweries, a family brewpub empire, home of North America's largest beer festival, and hops and barley crops that end up in Northwest beers.

PORTLAND

Portland is the capital of the Northwest microbrewing world. The city is home of eight breweries including regional Blitz-Weinhard, seven microbreweries and brewpubs, and countless taverns dispensing the Northwest's finest ales.

Portland has the distinction of having the most breweries of any city in North America. The Rose City is also home of the McMenamin brothers' empire of 10 brewpubs and 12 restaurants that serve Northwest craft beers. Mike and Brian McMenamin opened their first brewpub, the Hillsdale Brewery and Public House, in October 1985. Their 10th, the Edgefield Brewery, opened in Troutdale 20 miles east of Portland in February 1991.

The Northwest's first microbrewery opened in 1980 and since then Portland has never lacked for flavorful craft beers. Plagued by bad beer and tax problems, the Cartwright Brewery closed in 1982 after making the beachhead safe for the Widmers, Portland, and Bridgeports that followed.

A traveler to Portland could visit most of the city's brewpubs in the Northwest section on a leisurely afternoon. The day could begin with an early lunch at the Bridgeport Brewpub on Marshall Street, followed by a walk for a beer at Portland Brewing on Flanders Street, and a stroll by the Blitz-Weinhard Brewery.

Across from Blitz-Weinhard on West Burnside is Powell's Books, one of the most well-stocked bookstores in America. After picking up some books at Powell's, a visitor can stroll downtown for dinner at B. Moloch's/The Heathman Bakery & Pub on S.W. Salmon which shares the corner with a branch of the Widmer Brewery.

B. Moloch's is one of those special restaurants that celebrates dining with regional architecture and art. Although the Widmer Brewery and B. Moloch's are separate operations, they share customers in an interesting way. A glass wall separates the brewery and customers can watch the brewer working while they enjoy lunch or dinner. The paintings on the wall were by a French caricaturist who was commissioned to paint for the 1889 Paris Centennial Exposition. The food at B. Moloch's is also special -- baked goods and pizza cooked in a wood burning oven, smoked sausages, and smoked fish from Northwest waters.

OREGON BREWPUB CRAWL

An Oregon brewery adventure may take a couple days, but its worth the time to enjoy the state's natural wonders. Several brewpub crawls are possible. One is to spend a leisurely day or two visiting Portland's breweries and head out toward the Eastern flatlands along the Old Columbia River Highway. Half way there you'll reach the Hood River Brewery.

Along the Columbia River, wind surfers from all over the world try the treacherous winds on the gorge. After visiting Hood River Brewery, head south to I-5. All the way to the California border are a dozen towns like Corvallis, Bend, Ashland, and Newport that have a local brewpub or microbrewery.

The McMenamin's establishments in north-central Oregon provide numerous opportunities to visit neighborhood brewpubs and taverns to enjoy local color, good food, and microbrewed beers. Stop at several; they're a hospitable, low-key way to meet another Oregon resource -- its people.

OREGON BREWERS FESTIVAL

The third weekend in July finds Oregon celebrating its beer heritage with the Oregon Brewers Festival in Portland's Waterfront Park. The Widmer, Bridgeport, and Portland Breweries pool resources and arrange the event that draws 25,000 beer lovers for the three-day event. Portland's restaurants provide food, bands play during the daytime, and volunteers from the Oregon Brew Crew homebrew club pour beer from 40 Northwest microbreweries.

Plan to spend the third weekend in July in Portland to celebrate the festive marriage of good beer, food, and Northwest hospitality. You'll have plenty of stories to tell your friends and neighbors, and memories to last for years. You'd have to go to Munich's Oktoberfest to find a comparable event.

OREGON

BAY FRONT BREWERY AND PUBLIC HOUSE
748 Bay Boulevard
Newport 97365 503-265-3188

President: Jack L. Joyce
Brewmasters: John Maier and Greg Kebkey

Bay Front is one of Oregon's newest brewpubs, having opened in May 1989, with Governor Neil Goldschmidt cutting the ribbon. Newport is on the waterfront along Oregon's rocky coastline where long lines of tourists' cars trek every summer.

Bay Front's attractive nautical decor uses old brass tap handles and beer engines from the extinct Big Elk Tavern. Several items on the menu are made from beer, including pizza crust, ale-brewed chili with grated Oregon cheddar, beer cheese soup, and Pacific oysters with ale sauce. Live music is featured on Friday nights; a popular act is Mr. Bill's Traveling Trivia Show.

Brewer John Maier is a graduate of the Seibel Institute in Chicago and was named American Home Brewer of the Year in 1988 for his Oregon Special Barley Wine.

Brewpub menu: chili, soup, sandwiches, and pizza

Newporter
Rogue Smoke
Rogue Golden
Oatmeal Stout

1989: 600 barrels
1990: 1,000 barrels

BRIDGEPORT BREWPUB
1313 NW Marshall
Portland 97209 03-241-7179
President: Karl Ockert

Bridgeport is an example of how an urban redevelopment project can take an industrial warehouse and turn it into a comfortable brewpub with atmosphere. Bridgeport's bare brick walls, exposed timbers and open spaces create a neighborhood pub ambiance where one meets neighbors, professionals, tourists, students, and passersby for a fresh beer or pizza. It's a vast improvement from the carry-out beer and pizza joints that are too common.

Bridgeport brews several cask-conditioned ales that are immensely popular in the Northwest. Its large production (more than 8,000 barrels in 1990) makes it one of the largest brewpubs in North America (neighboring Hood River has the largest production in the state). Bridgeport's menu is limited to pizzas and foccatio Italian bread made from left-over pizza dough with spices and sauces added.

Bridgeport artfully combines the casual atmosphere, popular but limited menu, and great beers that reflect what Northwest craft brewing supporters want in a brewpub.

Blue Heron Bitter - fruity, complex and mildly hoppy
BridgePort Ale
Double Stout

1989: 5,000 barrels
1990: 8,523 barrels

DESCHUTES BREWERY & PUBLIC HOUSE
1044 Bond Street
Bend   97701   503-382-9242
President: Gary Fish
Brewer: John Harris

Deschutes opened in June 27, 1988, on the Western slope of the Cascades in Bend. Although Bend is off the beaten path for travelers making their way up and down I-5, it is a popular destination for Northwest craft brewing followers. Brewer John Harris, who plays the washboard at weekend jam sessions, specializes in producing specialty beers. His repertoire includes Cascade Golden Ale, Bachelor Bitter, Black Butte Porter, Mirror Pond Pale Ale, Jubelale, Obsidian Stout, Bond Street Brown Ale, Year Beer, Broken Top Bock, Wychick Weizen, Oktoberfest, Old Samhain, Winter Solstice Spiced Ale, and Metolious Spring Beer.

An indication of the popularity of Deschutes beers is that its Special Pilsener was the first beer to run out at the Oregon Brewers Festival in Portland in July 1990. Portland beer writer Fred Eckhardt rates Deschutes' Jubelale one of his favorite seasonal beers.

Deschutes kegs are distributed to restaurants and taverns in central Oregon, Portland, and the Willamette Valley.

Brewpub menu: pubfare

1989: 1,120 barrels
1990: 2,360 barrels

EUGENE CITY BREWING
P. O. Box 1182
Eugene   97401   503-895-3431
President: John Karlik
Equipment: Contract brewed at Kessler in Montana

HOOD RIVER BREWERY
506 Columbia Street
Hood River   97037   503-386-2281
President: Roger Barry
Brewer: James Emmerson

Hood River Brewery was founded in 1987 by five friends who claim, seven years later, that they are still friends. Brewer James Emmerson was graduated from Indiana's Butler University in 1963 with a double major in organic chemistry and German. He spent a year in Munich studying lager brewing and graduated from the Siebel Institute with a Masters in Brewing Technology.

Hood River is located on the Columbia River Gorge east of Portland. Wind sailers from around the world travel every summer to Hood River to try their skill on the windy Columbia River Gorge. Hood River's brewpub is called WhiteCap which is what patrons see when they look out the window at the windsurfers tacking across the treacherous waters.

Hood River received two gold medals at the 1989 Great American Beer Festival and was named Oregon Beer of the Year in 1987. It was the first Oregon microbrewery to bottle and had the state's largest microbrewery production in 1990 (more than 14,000 barrels).

Reggae and blues groups play at the WhiteCap on summer weekends when sailboarders congregate for their runs on the gorge.

Brewpub menu: pubfare

Full Sail Golden Ale - *brewed with 2-row pale and caramel malt; Hallertau and Tettnang hops*

Full Sail Amber Ale - *brewed with 2-row pale, caramel, and chocolate malts, Cascade and Halltertau hops*

Full Sail Brown Ale - *brewed with 2-row pale, caramel, and chocolate malts; East Kent Goldings and Willamette hops*

1989: 8,030 barrels
1990: 14,089 barrels

MCMENAMIN'S BREWPUBS

CORNELIUS PASS ROADHOUSE
Sunset Highway & Cornelius Pass Road
Hillsboro   97123   503-640-6174
1989: 89 barrels
1990: 500 barrels

EDGEFIELD BREWERY
2126 Southwest Halsey Street
Troutdale   97060   503-667-4352

FULTON PUB AND BREWERY
618 SW Nebraska
Portland   97201   503-246-9530
1989: 49 barrels
1990: 1,040 barrels

HIGHLAND PUB AND BREWERY
4225 SE 182nd Avenue
Gresham   97030   503-665-3015
1989: 66 barrels
1990: 1,040 barrels

HIGH STREET PUB
1243 High Street
Eugene   97401   503-345-4905
1989: 36 barrels
1990: 500 barrels

HILLSDALE BREWERY & PUBLIC HOUSE
1505 SW Sunset Boulevard
Portland   97201   503-246-3938
1989: 52 barrels
1990: 500 barrels

LIGHTHOUSE BREWPUB
4157 North Highway 101
Lincoln City   97367   503-994-7238
1989: 57 barrels
1990: 500 barrels

MCMENAMIN'S
6179 SW Murray Boulevard
Beaverton   97005   503-644-4562
1990: 600 barrels

OAK HILLS BREWPUB
14740 NW Cornell Road
Portland   97229   503-645-0286
1990: 200 barrels

THOMPSON BREWERY & PUBLIC HOUSE
3575 Liberty Road South
Salem   97302   503-363-7286
1989: 58 barrels
1990: 1,040 barrels

Mike and Brian McMenamin run a brewpub empire in northern Oregon. Among their two dozen taverns in the Portland area are 10 brewpubs with more on the way. All of the McMenamin's establishments have at least 20 taps to carry their beers as well as a selection from other Northwest craft breweries.

The McMenamins opened Oregon's first brewpub in October 1985 at the Hillsdale Brewery and Public House. Brewing was done in Captain Neon's Fermentation Chamber decorated with day-glo colors and off-beat art work. It wasn't just freshly-brewed beer that attracted customers.

The McMenamins had fun during the start-up days experimenting with brewing concoctions that included raspberries, blueberries, pears, pineapples, rhubarb, apples -- and Mars candy bars! They claim the Mars bar slipped into a brewing vessel by accident, but the incident insured them of publicity for years afterwards.

Pacific Northwest grains and whole Oregon hops are used in McMenamin's beers which are keg-conditioned, unfiltered, and unpasteurized. While some larger breweries strive for uniformity, the McMenamins enjoy interesting varieties from batch to batch. "The only rule in our brewery is that there are no rules," is how their literature describes their philosophy.

Cascade Head Ale - named after the meadow at the top of the Cascades 1,000 feet above Lincoln City; lightest McMenamin ale brewed with Halltertauer hops

Ruby - Oregon raspberries are used to create the ruby color and tart flavor; a unique product

Crystal Ale - named after the old Crystal Ballroom in Portland and the grain roasted to create amber color and caramel flavor

Terminator - the best selling McMenamin beer despite the fact that it has three times the calories and alcohol content of conventional beers; brewed with four malts and 2 hops;

Hammerhead - dark amber, brewed with two types of crystal malts and Cascade hops

OREGON TRAIL
341 SW Second Street
Corvallis 97330 503-758-3527

President/Brewer: Jerry Shadomy
Equipment: 7-barrel brew kettle from Hart Brewing

Jerry Shadomy was one of Oregon's pioneer microbrewers opening his downtown Corvallis microbrewery in July 1987. Corvallis is located in the central Willamette Valley and is the home of Oregon State University. Although Oregon Trail was one of Oregon's first microbreweries, its growth has not paralleled the state's more well-known microbreweries. Distribution has been a problem and Shadomy continues to self-distribute.

Oregon Trail's three-floor, gravity-fed system is shoehorned into the downtown Old Town Center shopping arcade. The top floor houses sacks of 2-row Klages malt and a malt hopper. Grain is milled and lowered into the mash tun on the second floor where Shadomy has his office. After mashing, wort is lowered to the copper brewkettle on the first floor for the boiling.

The Old World Deli next to the brewery is one of Oregon Trail's best accounts. Postal workers from the post office next door stop by the deli for a fresh Oregon Trail Ale after hours. Portland beer writer Fred Eckhardt rates

Oregon Trail's Chinook Stout and Winter Porter as some of his favorite seasonal beers.

Oregon Trail Ale - an amber ale

Oregon Trail Porter - brewed with a combination of five malts to produce a complex flavor resembling a sweet, nutty coffee

Extra Stout XX - brewed with Chinook and Tettnanger hops and chocolate malt

1989: 131 barrels
1990: N/A

PIZZA DELI AND BREWERY
249 Redwood Highway
Cave Junction 97523 503-592-3556

President: Jerry Miller
Brewer: Hubert Smith

Jerry Miller owns a pizza restaurant in Cave Junction near the Oregon coastline a few miles from the California border. Cave Junction is a logging community in the heart of the giant Redwoods a few miles north of the Redwood National Forest. Miller's Pizza Deli is on a two-lane stretch of the Redwood Highway crammed with logging trucks.

Miller had read about Portland's brewpubs and consulted with a local filmmaker, Hubert Smith, who writes about specialty beers for Northwest publications. Smith's "weakness" is English-style, cask-conditioned ales.

Miller and Smith put together a plan to open a small brewpub in Miller's Pizza Deli and they started brewing in the summer of 1990. Smith designed the brewing system from locally made equipment.

Miller's son operates a second Pizza Deli a few miles away in Brookings Harbor on the coast. A second brewpub in the family may be in the works.

Brewpub menu: pizza, pubfare

1990: 80 barrels (began brewing in August 1990)

PORTLAND BREWING
1339 N.W. Flanders
Portland   97209   503-222-7150
President: Fred Bowman
Brewmaster: Art Larrance

In 1986, two Portland businessmen, Fred Bowman and Art Larrance, fell in love with the idea of starting a small brewery in Portland just as the Northwest microbrewing movement was beginning. They began brewing in the Northwest warehouse area of Portland which is now home to several microbreweries, taverns and restaurants.

Portland Brewing is an American pub complete with bar towels, dart boards, friendly publicans, fresh ales and short orders. The brewery equipment is visible on the second floor a few feet from the bar. In addition to brewing their own beers, Portland brews Grant's ales under license.

In early 1990, Portland Brewing purchased the old Armour meat packing building behind the warehouse to expand. They will add a bottling line to sell their beers in the retail market. Two new beers appeared in 1990: Portland HB (House Bitter) and Portland Porter.

Portland Brewing is one of the sponsors of the annual Oregon Brewers Festival in July.

Brewpub menu: pubfare

Oregon Dry - *pale, light ale brewed with honey, Nugget and Willamette hops; the honey is almost entirely fermented and leaves a slight honey flavor*

Portland Ale - *pale ale made with Nugget and Cascade hops*

Portland HB (House Bitter) - *a golden ale*

Portland Porter - *black, malty beer with a creamy head*

Timberline Classic Ale - *amber ale brewed to celebrate the 50th anniversary of the Timberline Lodge on Mt. Hood; pale and caramel malt and Nugget hops produce a mildly nutty flavor*

1989: 3,100 barrels
1990: N/A

ROGER'S ZOO
2037 Sherman Avenue
North Bend   97459   503-756-1463
President/Brewer: Roger Scott

First-time visitors to Roger's Zoo on the lower end of Sherman Avenue might be intimidated by the dilapidated condition of the neighborhood. Patrons seem to have wandered over after an appearance at the courthouse nearby. Charitably, this is not North Bend's most prestigious section.

Once inside Roger's Zoo, the appearance might lead one to ponder that the workmen haven't finished with much-needed repairs. A dishwasher stands next to a pool table whose coin-operating mechanism is broken. Overhead hang advertisements, flyers, and what-not in no perceived manner of organization or reasoning. The floor is dusty, the chairs don't match, and a fresh coat of paint never seems to have graced the walls.

But Roger's Zoo is crowded almost every day with patrons ranging from jurists, lawyers, and legal clerks who have wandered over from the courthouse (presumably with some of their clients), to the unemployed, loggers, and blue-collar workers. Everyone, it seems, has heard that Roger provides his own entertainment along with microbrewed beer, fresh pizza, and killer nachos. "In my zoo I've got elephants, giraffes, panthers, and the mouse sitting over in the corner that hides," Roger Scott was quoted when asked how he describes his clientele.

Roger Scott talked North Bend's city officials into taking over a run-down restaurant so he could start a brewpub in an area of town that had seen better days. In two years, he has built such a following that the Portland Oregonian, the state's largest newspaper, wrote a feature story praising his exotic mixture of people, pizza, pilsener and personality.

Brewpub menu: pizza, pubfare

Zoo Brew - *whatever Roger brewed last*

1990: 6 barrels

ROGUE BREWERY & PUBLIC HOUSE
31 B Water Street
Ashland   97520   503-488-5061
President: Jack L. Joyce
Brewmaster: Michael Eaton

When the Rogue's oceanside brewpub opened in October 1988, a regional magazine claimed it was "perhaps the nation's most beautiful brewery site,"

RAW MATERIAL

where it was possible to watch salmon swimming along the rocky coastline while sipping fresh Rogue ales.

The Rogue is enclosed by a park on one side, a creek on the other, and Water Street in the front. The Rogue's sister brewery, the Bay Front in Newport, is also on the waterfront.

The Rogue brews with Oregon malting barley and hops. Several seasonal beers are brewed around the year: Logger Ale, Rogue-n-Berry, Rogue Smoke, and Golden Coast. Rogue's ales are served in western Oregon taverns and restaurants.

Rogue Golden - *golden, malty ale made with Oregon and Munich malt and Willamette hops*
Ashland Amber - *brewed with Oregon malts and Cascade hops*
Shakespeare Stout - *chocolatey, mellow stout; 6% alcohol brewed with four barley malts, organic oatmeal, Tettnang and Cascade hops*

1989: 800 barrels
1990: 500 barrels

WIDMER BREWERY #1
929 N. Russell
Portland 97209 503-221-0631
President/Brewer Kurt Widmer
Equipment: JV Northwest

WIDMER BREWERY #2
923 SW 9th Street
Portland 97205   503-221-0631 (B. Moloch restaurant)
Brewer: Frank Commanday
Brewery equipment: JV Northwest

Widmer is the only family-owned and operated microbrewery in Portland. Father Ray and brothers Kurt and Rob began brewing in 1985 and have made their brewery one of the finest in the Northwest.

Kurt Widmer studied brewing in Dusseldorf where he learned how to brew the old German-style alt beer as well as bock and seasonal beers. Widmer's

special yeast strains were obtained from the Brewing Research Institute at Weihenstephan in Bavaria.

In the spring of 1990, Widmer moved from its original site in Northwest Portland near the city's other microbreweries across the Willamette River into a refurbished historic building. The new brewery's capacity will be 28,000 barrels per year.

A second Widmer location shares space with the stylish B. Moloch's Bakery and Pub in downtown Portland. The restaurant features Widmer's beer along with other popular Northwest beers. Although technically not a brewpub, Widmer's second location is another example of the creativity and flexibility in the microbrewing industry. Look for restaurants to explore the concept of co-locating with a microbrewery that does not have its own brewpub.

Widmer Altbier - copper-colored, brewed with four malts and two Northwest hops

Widmer Weizen - light, spritzy, and brewed with half wheat malt and Tettanger hops grown in Oregon

Widmer Hefeweizen - unfiltered Weizenbier, a traditional German-style beer popular in the summer

Festbier - caramel-colored, malty, smooth Christmas beer

Oktoberfest - amber, malty seasonal beer brewed with Hallertau hops

Bock - golden and full-bodied; brewed with four malts and three hops

Maerzenbier - brewed in the fall for springtime drinking

1989: 7,800 barrels
1990: 12,000 barrels

THE SOUTHWEST

MICROBREWERIES BLOOMING IN THE DESERT

The area that has been the latest to join the microbrewing revolution extends Westward of the Rio Grande River all the way to the Pacific Ocean. Although this is one of the most dynamic economic regions in North America, its late arrival to the ranks of active microbrewing has less to do with the economy than the paucity of breweries before Prohibition.

Brewing in America, after all, had largely been concentrated in Eastern and Midwestern industrial cities of Pittsburgh, New York, Chicago, Milwaukee, and St. Louis, and later expanded to several Western cities earlier in this century. The areas of the country that had the least active brewing industry were the Southeast and Southwest.

Hot weather has never been a boon to brewing. Before the invention of modern refrigeration and the widespread use of refrigerated tank cars, beer was brewed and consumed in a small marketing area.

ALL SHADES UNDER THE SUN

Although the desert Southwest was late to catch on to the microbrewing trend, the growth has been quick to catch up with the other Western areas like the Northwest and Rocky Mountain states. Most of the Southwestern microbreweries are less than three years old, and they range from the multi-million dollar Eureka Brewing in downtown Los Angeles to quirky Arizona hideaway places like Crazy Ed's Black Mountain Brewery in Cave Creek and the downright eccentric Electic Dave Brewery in a South Bisbee garage north of the Mexico border.

More typical, however, are upscale brewpubs like Hops and Barley's in Phoenix, and Southern California's Alpine Village, Fullerton Hofbrau, and Columbia Grill. In the competitive restaurant market, these brewpubs are going after the high-end customer who demands excellent cuisine with freshly brewed beers. This is the most lucrative branch of microbrewing and the one that entrepreneurs are recognizing in Atlanta, Chicago, Seattle, and Los Angeles. Money spent on developing a restaurant clientele is the smartest way to develop a business plan for a successful brewpub.

Microbreweries of various stripes have started in Phoenix, Los Angeles, San Diego, and dusty desert towns of New Mexico, Arizona, California, and Nevada. New ventures will be coming on stream soon in rural outposts, mountain resorts, and bustling suburban centers.

In 1987, the Arizona legislature passed a bill legalizing brewpubs. The initiative was sponsored by two Phoenix-area entrepreneurs interested in starting microbreweries. Nevertheless, others jumped in and within three years the state had eight microbreweries with more planned. The movement was somewhat typical for the 30 states that have legalized microbreweries since California became the first in 1982. Interest in microbreweries has been so strong that as soon as state legislatures legalize craft breweries, the ink on the governer's signature is hardly dry before eager brewers are opening their doors to let customers taste locally brewed beer.

Chef Russell Hodges sliding a gourmet pizza into an Italian-made, wood-burning stove at Scottsdale's HOPS Brewpub.

San Diego, which once had four breweries (Mission, Balboa, Aztec, and San Diego), has become the latest Southwestern city to embrace the microbrewing movement. Already, the city boasts two brewpubs -- Old Columbia and Callahan's -- and the Mission microbrewery. Old Columbia is planning expansion to La Jolla, Mission Beach, and State College area.

San Diego's first microbrewery, Bolt Brewery, opened in 1987 but closed within the year despite favorable reviews.

MICROBREWING BONANZA COMING IN THE SOUTHWEST

For a variety of reasons, the microbrewing revolution should find its most active and successful growth in the Southwest. The demographics in the country have been shifting southward and westward for the last three decades. As the 1990 census revealed, California, Arizona, and New Mexico are destined for explosive growth in population as well as in the computer, electronics, aerospace, and defense industries.

The microbrewing revolution has already established a beach-head in San Diego, Phoenix, and Los Angeles; look for Tucson, Santa Fe, Albuquerque, Flagstaff, Las Vegas, and Reno to join the ranks as well as ventures in desert towns blossoming throughout the Southwest.

ARIZONA

BANDERSNATCH BREWPUB
125 5th Street
Tempe   85281   602-966-4438
Co-owners: Joe Risi, Joe Mocca
Brewer: Clark Nelson
Equipment: 7-barrel JV Northwest

Arizona's first brewpub opened on the campus of Arizona State in June 1988 after the state legislature changed the law to permit a brewery to operate as a retailer. Phoenix reportedly is the fourth largest beer consuming city in the country.

Joe Risi bought the campus tavern that became Arizona's first brewpub because it is located a few blocks from the stadium where the Arizona State Sun Devils and Phoenix Cardinals play football. On game days, Bandersnatch opens three hours before kick off to accommodate thirsty students, alumni, and fans. The brewpub seats 75 with "standing room for 1,200 on football weekends," according to Risi.

Customers can be initiated into Bandersnatch's Beer in Your Face Club by having a mug of beer tossed in their face; you get to keep the mug and a T-shirt for your troubles.

Bandersnatch, which won the *New Times* Best of Phoenix award for draft beer in 1989, was the first Arizona microbrewery to bottle beer. Risi opened his second brewpub, Barley's, in Phoenix and plans to open a chain of brewpubs nationwide in the future. Bandersnatch makes its own root beer.

Brewpub menu: pubfare, burgers, appetizers and pasta

Cardinal Ale - English-style pale ale
Big Horn Premium Ale - English-style bitters
Bandersnatch Milk Stout - a sweet stout

1989: 360 barrels
1990: 435 barrels

BARLEY'S BREWPUB
4883 N. 20th Street
Phoenix   85016   602-241-9030

Owner: Joe Risi
Brewer: Ivan Loveless
Equipment: 14-barrel Pub Brewing system

Barley's is the second Phoenix-area brewpub opened by Joe Risi. It is located in a shopping mall at 20th & Camelback in affluent northeast Phoenix.

Barley's opened March 30, 1990 and will begin bottling 750 ml. bottles in the summer of 1991. Barley's won the *New Times* Best of Phoenix award for best brewpub and best draft beer in 1990.

The atmosphere in the 110-year old building is classic saloon with mahogany back bar, tin ceiling, flagstone floors, and murals on the walls. The brewpub seats 140 inside and another 100 on the outdoor patio.

Brewpub menu: lunches, dinners, appetizers

Trick - a light ale
Fair Dinkum - an amber ale
Toby Stout
1990: 400 barrels

CRAZY ED'S BLACK MOUNTAIN BREWING
P.O. Box 1940
Cave Creek   85331   602-488-2609

Co-owners: Ed and Maria Chilleen
Brewer: Eric Schalk
Equipment: Used German equipment

Crazy Ed's Black Mountain Brewery is in the community of Cave Creek, a two-hour drive north of Phoenix. The last part of a drive to Cave Creek is over winding roads through Arizona's scenic desert. The microbrewery is operated by Ed and Maria Chilleen at their Satisfied Frog Restaurant, a popular spot for tourists and week-end trippers looking for the offbeat experience.

The Chileens met Georg Arnold of the Brauerie Arnold on a vacation to Germany in 1987 and hired him to come to Arizona to build their brewery and produce German-style lagers. The Black Mountain Brewery opened in January 1989, next door to the Satisfied Frog at a cost of $500,000.

Crazy Ed's pilsener won a bronze medal at the 1990 Great American Beer Festival in Denver in the American pilsener category.

Arizona Pilsener
Black Mountain Gold
Frog Light
1989: 53 barrels
1990: 3,200 barrels

ELECTRIC DAVE BREWERY
1A DD Street
South Bisbee 85603   602-432-3606
President/Brewmaster: Dave Harvan
Equipment: Locally designed and made; Cross storage tanks

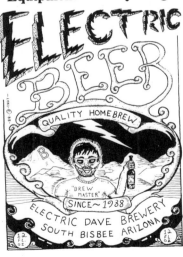

Dave Harvan was a construction worker when he decided to build his own brewery. His previous brewing experience included 11 years as a dedicated homebrewer and a term as president of the Suds of the Pioneers homebrew club.

Harvan had his brew kettle, mash tun, fermenters, and cooling system fabricated locally in Bisbee, a town of 8,000, located 100 miles southeast of Tucson. Since he did much of the construction work himself, Harvan said his investment was only $20,000 to build the brewery.

He received his license in January 1988 and opened a year later in a converted garage south of Bisbee. Electric Dave's beers vary from batch to batch ranging from standard ales and pilseners to weiss, helles, and porter. Distribution is restricted to southeastern Arizona with plans to extend to Tucson. Harvan offers tours of the brewery and recommends "bringing your daughter."

Electric Dave's Pilsener
Electric Dave's Porter

1989: 60 barrels
1990: 330 barrels

HOPS BREWERY
Scottsdale Fashion Square
7000 Camelback Road
Scottsdale 85281 602-645-HOPS

President: Roy Hoover
Brewer: Julius Hummer
Equipment: JV Northwest, Grundy cellar tanks

Hops is a 400-seat brewpub, restaurant, and beer garden which opened New Years Day 1990, in the prestigous Fashion Square mall in the Phoenix suburb of Scottsdale. Although Hops is a brewpub, it is promoting itself as a specialty restaurant to appeal to affluent Scottsdale consumers who include some of the wealthiest people in the Southwest.

General Manager Roy Hoover designed an elegant menu with chef Russell Hodges and cookbook writer Anne Greet. Their aim was to establish Hops as a fine dining establishment which also happens to brew its own beer. Hops has a main dining room, beer garden, and granite bar in the lounge. Hops beers are available only at the brewpub.

Brewmaster Julius Hummer's father started Boulder Brewing, Colorado's first microbrewery. Hummer previously worked in English, German, and American breweries before coming to Scottsdale. His beer recipes have won numerous medals at the Great American Beer Festival.

Brewpub menu: selections from Californian, Italian and Oriental cuisines with appetizers, salads, pastas, sandwiches, pizzas, and calzones

Pale Ale
Bock
Oktoberfest
Nut Brown Ale
Barley Wine
Weizen
1990: 1,200 barrels

CALIFORNIA

ALPINE VILLAGE HOFBRAU
833 W. Torrance Boulevard
Torrance 90502   213-329-8881

President: Guenther Buerk
Brewer: M. Velas

Alpine Village brewpub is located in a shopping arcade with 30 Old World shops selling products from Europe. With a 10,000-barrel capacity, Alpine Village is the largest microbrewery in Southern California. The brewpub features a beer garden, restaurant, and German music for special events.

Alpine Village is affiliated with the Hofbrauhaus Traunstein, a Bavarian brewery that traces it origins to the early 1700s. Gunther Buerk also owns the Fullerton Hofbrau near the Fullerton College campus. Alpine Village's slogan is "The best microbrewery this side of Bavaria;" its colors are blue and white, the colors of Bavaria. Oktoberfest begins in early September and lasts until the end of October. Alpine Village's beers are sold in kegs as well as 2-liter ceramic-topped bottles.

Alpine Village Hofbrau Lager
Alpine Village Hofbrau Light
Alpine Village Hofbrau Pilsener
Alpine Village Hofbrau Winter Bock
1989: 700 barrels
1990: N/A

ANGELES BREWING
10009 Conoga Avenue
Chatsworth   91311   818-407-0340

President: Richard Belliveau
1989: 6 barrels
1990: 750 barrels

BELMONT BREWING
25 39th Place
Long Beach   90803   213-433-3891

President: David Lott
Brewer: David Hansen

Belmont Brewing is another California first -- the first brewpub on the beach. Located near Belmont Shores and next to the pier, Belmont includes a beachfront brewpub and outdoor beer garden. Belmont opened in the summer of 1989.

Marathon Ale
Full Sail Ale
Fog Cutter
Long Beach Crude
1990: 520 barrels

BREWHOUSE GRILL/STATE STREET BREWING
202 State Street
Santa Barbara 93101   805-963-3090

President: Fred Kukulus
Brewer: Mark Safarik

Santa Barbara is known for its beaches, nightlife, and excellent restaurants. The town's first brewpub, the Brewhouse Grill and State Street Brewing, opened in the summer of 1990 and is a five-minute walk from the beach.

The Brewhouse Grill is a saloon with brass fans, heavy wood furniture, and old photos on the walls from Santa Barbara's historic past. Owner Fred Kukulus also started the 8,000 ft. high Mammoth Lakes Brewery in the Mammoth Lakes resort near the Nevada border.

The Brewhouse Grill's small brewery capacity (10 barrel system) requires that some of their beers be brewed at the Alpine Village Brewpub in Torrance.

Brewpub menu: German dishes, complete dinners and pubfare

Anacapa Ale

Mission Creek Porter

City Lager

1990: (opened summer of 1990)

BUTTERFIELD BREWING
777 East Olive Avenue
Fresno   93704   209-264-5521
President: Jeff Wolpert
Brewer: Kevin Cox
Equipment: JV Northwest

Butterfield Brewing is a bit more formal than most brewpubs. Customers are greeted by a receptionist and shown to their seats, often by owner Jeff Wolpert. A veteran restaurateur, Wolpert considers Butterfield a place to dine first, and a brewpub second.

The brewpub is named after the Butterfield Overland Express Stage Company, which carried passengers and mail from St. Louis to San Francisco in the mid-1800s. Wolpert is a descendant of the founder of the company. Butterfield regularly produces a light ale, red ale, and porter as well as specialty beers that are rotated every 10 to 14 days.

Brewpub menu: beer-steamed shrimp boiled in a mixture of spices and the brewery's porter

San Joaquin Golden Ale - *brewed with Cascade hops and slightly on the sweet side; it's the brewery's biggest seller*

Bridalveil Ale - *brewed with a mixture of five hop varieties, dominated by Northern Brewers and Chinook hops*

Tower Dark Ale - *gold medal winner for porter at 1989 GABF; roasted malts are used sparingly to produce a hearty, dark ale*

1989: 600 barrels
1990: 850 barrels

CALLAHAN'S PUB & BREWING
8280-A Mira Mesa Boulevard
San Diego   92126   619-578-7892
Co-Owners: Scott Stamp, Lee Doxtader
Brewer: Scott Stamp

Callahan's was an Irish pub in San Diego's Mira Mesa Mall when homebrewers Lee Doxtader and Scott Stamp decided to add a brewery to their pub. They served their first beer, Callahan's Red, in June 1990.

Callahan's lively clientele are attracted to the fresh beer as well as the pub's dart boards, TV, rock and roll jukebox, and neighborhood atmosphere. Callahan's two beers are named after the carpet colors of the upscale restaurant that preceded Callahan's. Part of the rich oak paneling was replaced by glass partitions to show the brewery's stainless steel equipment. Brewery capacity is 350 barrels a year.

Brewpub menu: Irish pubfare including "bangers and mash"

Callahan's Red
Callahan's Gold
1990: (opened in June 1990)

CENTRAL COAST BREWING
3432-A Roberto Court
San Luis Obispo   93401   805-541-5883
President: David Braun

Central Coast opened in 1990 and sells kegs only in the county.
1990: 335 barrels

CROWN CITY BREWERY
300 South Raymond Avenue
Pasadena 91105   818-577-5548
President/Brewer: Mike Lanzarotta

Fine Foods & Ales

Crown City is the brainchild of four childhood friends who combined their talents to start their brewpub: marketing expert Dennis Hartman, accountant Jack Robinson, brewer Mike Lanzarotta and chef Bob Talbott. The brewpub features a 30-foot polished oak wood bar, 200-gallon copper brewing tanks on display behind glass, and a collection of over 800 bottles above the bar.

Crown City's menu lists over 150 beers from 32 countries and microbreweries. Once patrons have sampled 100 beers, they receive a T-shirt and get their name engraved on a commemorative plaque hung in the bar.

Brewmaster Lanzarotta produces a wheat beer, amber ale, and a stout, as well as seasonal brews like Father Christmas Wassail, a spiced ale.

Crown City publishes a chatty newsletter, *Talk of the Crown,* which contains staff news, a schedule of upcoming events, and beer trivia. A recent edition noted that an English pub offered customers, for $8,000, the privilege of having their ashes interred beneath their favorite bar stool where their friends could toast them daily. Crown City offers the same service for $7,000 (payable in advance).

Brewpub menu: pubfare, select dinners

Mt. Wilson Wheat - German Weizen brewed with one-fourth malted wheat; a fruity, golden-colored beer enjoyed with a slice of lemon and named for the prominent peak overlooking the city

Arroyo Amber Ale - English pale ale named for the riverbed that runs under the Pasadena Freeway

Black Cloud Oatmeal Stout - brewed with six types of malted and unmalted barley, along with rolled oats; described as having a "creamy, roasted flavor with a spicy finish"

1989: 600 barrels
1990: 308 barrels

FIRESTONE AND FLETCHER BREWING CO.
P.O. Box 244
Los Olivos   93441   805-688-3940

President: Brooks Firestone
Brewer: Hale Fletcher

Brooks Firestone would like to see American bars embrace the English custom of the spacer -- a non-alcoholic drink served every third or fourth round to keep customers from drinking too much alcohol too fast.

Instead, Firestone has rolled out the non-alcoholic beverage. Heir to the tire company and owner of a Santa Ynez Valley vineyard, he's also president of the only microbrewery in the country devoted to producing non-alcoholic beer. To be considered non-alcoholic, beer must contain less than 0.5% alcohol by volume. Some brewers simply "de-alcoholize" beer, boiling away the alcohol with a vacuum distillation process. Firestone says this damages the flavor.

With the assistance of biochemist Hale Fletcher and Dr. Michael Lewis, head of UC Davis brewing school, Firestone has developed a brewing process in which no alcohol is produced during fermentation. In an August 1988 tasting of non-alcoholic beers, the *Los Angeles Times* rated Firestone ahead of popular imports Kaliber, Clausthaler, and Moussy.

Says Firestone of his potential market: "Ten million cases of non-alcoholic beer are sold annually, which is less than 1% of all beer sold. But my perception is that that tiny segment is very interesting and potentially profitable, even though it wouldn't be profitable to a regular brewery." Firestone's packaging was a finalist for a CLIO award in the 1989 non-alcoholic beverage package design category. Firestone's contains 75 calories per 12 oz. serving.

Firestone Non-alcoholic Brew - brewed from three kinds of two-row barley malts with no perservatives added. Described by the LA Times as "A dark-beer kind of aroma, slightly caramelized and rich; creamy, hoppy and relatively beer-like aftertaste. Not much bitterness."
1989: 3,000 barrels
1990: N/A

FULLERTON HOFBRAU
323 North State College Boulevard
Fullerton   92631   714-870-7400

President: Russell Brent
Brewer: Gunther Buerk
Equipment: Pilot brewery; used German equipment to be installed

Fullerton Hofbrau is one of southern California's latest entries into microbrewing and the second in Orange County after Heritage Brewing. The German word hofbrau means the royal court brewery. German proverbs like "Hopfen und Malz, Gott erhalt's" ("Hops and Malt, God preserve them!") are inscribed on the brewpub walls.

Fullerton Hofbrau offers authentic German cuisine such as wurst platters, Bavarian-style mustard, sauerkraut, rouladen, spaetzle (buttery dumplings), potato salad, and wienerschnitzel. Beer-steamed clams and fried tomatoes in beer batter topped with mozzarella are a few American specialties. Appetizers are wild game "speedies" -- pieces of marinated lamb and venison roasted on skewers over an open fire.

Fullerton is brewing with a pilot plant until new equipment imported from Germany is shipped. In the meantime, fresh beer is delivered from the Alpine Village Hofbrau which brewer Gunther Buerk founded in 1988. According to Buerk, Fullerton's equipment came from a brewery started by Bavarian Duke Maximilian in the early 1700s.

Entertainment and music are featured Monday through Saturday nights.

Brewpub menu: German and American foods including hamburgers, sandwiches, and salad bar

Kings Lager
Kings Light
Princes Pilsener
Knights Light

1990: (opened May 1990)

GORKY'S CAFE AND BREWERY
536 East Eighth Street
Los Angeles   90021   213-463-4060

President: Fred Powers
Brewer: Chris Quint

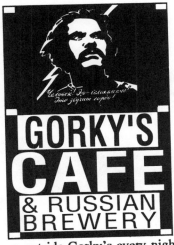

Glasnost may be faltering in the Soviet Union, but it's thriving in Los Angeles' theater district. In a popular bistro named Gorky's, patrons are eating authentic Russian dishes like borscht, piroshki, blintzes, and kasha in the Red Square Room and drinking Russian Imperial Stout brewed on the premises.

Gorky's has been compared to a Greenwich Village-style coffee house that attracts artists, musicians, writers, students, ethnic food lovers, and anyone else who likes to listen to Russian classical music, recite poetry, or drink espresso into the late hours. Whatever their interest, patrons line up outside Gorky's every night for the moderately priced food and exotic ambiance. Service is proletarian chic (cafeteria style).

Fred Powers' maternal and paternal grandparents came from Russia. When Powers bought Gorky's in 1985, he expanded from 3,000 to 10,000 sq. ft.

Gorky's breakfast specials can be as adventurous as Russian Oatmeal Raisin Pancakes and Karamazov omelettes (chicken livers, onions, mushrooms, sour cream, and caviar). Theater-goers can dine until 2 AM or all night long on the weekend. Prices are moderate, even for a downtown Los Angeles restaurant. Jazz groups play at night.

A second Gorky's has opened at the old Tick Tock restaurant in Hollywood at 1716 N. Cahuenga. Powers is pursuing a joint venture agreement to open a Gorky's brewpub in the Crimean resort town of Yalta.

Brewpub menu: Russian specialties; breakfasts, lunches, and dinners

Russian Imperial Stout
Baltic Light
Red Star Ale
Golden Pilsener

1989: N/A
1990: 1,750 barrels

HERITAGE BREWING
24921 Dana Point Harbor Drive
Dana Point   92629   714-240-2060

President: John Stoner
Brewer: Mark Mericle
Equipment: 10-barrel system designed by Jim Schleuter

Co-founders Mark Mericle and John Stoner were disenchanted Rockwell employees when they decided to get off the corporate ladder and pursue their interest in craft brewing. They designed a pilot brewery in Mark's garage in February 1988 and began scouting for sites and investors for their dream brewpub.

After searching in Costa Mesa and Irvine, they settled on Dana Point after a friend showed them the advantages of locating in the newly incorporated city in Orange County. Heritage is Orange County's first brewpub and claims one of the longest bars in a brewpub -- 82 feet long.

Brewer Mark Mericle traveled in Europe where he became enchanted with craft brewing. Later he served an apprenticeship with Jim Schleuter at Dead Cat Brewpub in Woodland. Schleuter designed Heritage's brewing system, copying his model for the Hogshead and Dead Cat brewpubs. Mericle brews several seasonal beers including an Irish red, summer wheat, holiday stout, and a strong ale. Heritage is available in 22 oz. bottles.

Brewpub menu: pubfare

Lantern Bay Blond

Sail Ale

Dana Porter

Heritage Specialty - brew of the week

1989: (opened in December 1989)
1990: 850 barrels

LOS ANGELES BREWING/EUREKA BREWERY
1845 South Bundy Drive
West Los Angeles   90025   213-207-1000
Co-owners: Wolfgang Puck, Barbara Lazaroff
Brewer: Mark Scott

The family team of chef Wolfgang Puck and restaurant designer Barbara Lazaroff are behind the Los Angeles Brewing/Eureka Brewpub, the West Coast's trendiest brewpub. Puck was the guiding force behind Spago's restaurant in Hollywood, Chinois on Main in Santa Monica, and Postrio in San Francisco. His other enterprises include his own food company which packages frozen pizza, and appearances on ABC's "Good Morning America" as guest chef.

Barbara Lazaroff used her restaurant design talents and gave Eureka a neo-industrial motif. Entrance is through enormous copper doors surrounded by glass block walls. The top of the 40-foot-long bar is hammered copper accented with perforated pewter panels. Eureka's other touches include sawtooth gears, rivets, and glazed tiles in the shape of sausages. Special lighting highlights the industrial features throughout the brewpub.

Brewer Mark Scott was graduated from UC-Davis with a degree in Fermentation Science and worked for Anheuser-Busch in Van Nuys and St. Louis. Eureka lager is bottled and kegged for off-premise sales. The brewery has a 12,000-barrel/year capacity with room to expand to 50,000 barrels. Eureka began brewing March 22, 1990; the restaurant opened in May.

The brewpub includes banquet facilities for 100, a gift shop, seating for 184 (34 in the bar), and is decorated with numerous works of art on consignment from local artists.

Brewpub menu: Asian, Latin, and European cuisine "with an American flair;" the menu changes seasonally

Eureka California Lager - brewed with 2-row Klages malt, Hallertau and Tettnang hops

1990: (opened in March 1990)

MAMMOTH LAKES BREWING
170 Mountain Boulevard
Mammoth Lakes 93546   619-934-8134
President: Fred Kukulus
Brewer: John Fogarty

Mammoth Lakes is a year-round resort north of L.A. and east of San Francisco near the Nevada border. Fred Kukulus founded the Mammoth Lakes Brewery in November 1988, after moving from Manhattan Beach.

At 8,000 feet elevation, Mammoth Lakes is the highest brewery in California. All of the beers brewed by John Fogarty are named after old gold mining towns that thrived in the area during the 1850s gold rush. Mammoth Lakes beers are available on draft and in liter bottles.

Kukulus and Fogarty also started the State Street Brewery in Santa Barbara's Brewhouse Grill, which opened in 1990.

Lundy Light
Dogtown Ale
Dogtown Ale
Bodie Bold Porter

1989: 375 barrels
1990: N/A

MISSION BREWING
1751 Hancock Street
San Diego   92110   619-294-3363
President: Bruce Kannenberg
Brewer: Clint Stromberg

The Mission Brewery Plaza was built in 1913 and is listed in the National Register of Historic Places. The plaza includes offices, retail space, a brewery, and a 250-seat restaurant

San Diego Amber
Mission Gold
Aztec Red

OBISPO BREWING
P.O. Box 981
San Luis Obispo   93406   805-543-0487
Co-owners: Mike Bailey, Rick Hamlin

OKIE GIRL BREWING
658 Lebec Road
Lebec   93243   805-248-6451
President: John Benson
Equipment: Custom fabricated, used dairy equipment

Lebec's Okie Girl brewpub is in a combination restaurant, gift shop, museum, playground, and brewery in the San Joaquin Valley made famous by John Steinbeck's *The Grapes of Wrath*. A former resident of the area, Wade McWhirter, reportedly was the subject of a photograph in a *Life* magazine story that inspired Steinbeck's character, Tom Joad.

Lebec is off Interstate 5 at the junction of the borders of Los Angeles and Ventura counties. The California Department of Transportation has not allowed Okie Girl to promote itself on a billboard because of the negative connotations of the term "Okie." The Okie Girl in this case is Mary Lynn Rasmussen, who was born in Broken Bow, Oklahoma, and works for the brewery.

Okie Girl's childrens' menu is a coloring book that tells the story of the Okies' move to California during the Depression. Artifacts in the brewpub include the head of a grizzly bear shot by Rasmussen's sister in Alaska.

Okie Girl originally was the Grapevine Brewery. The brewery also makes its own root beer named Old Ridge Route. Historical and tourist information about the area is published in a small newspaper, *Okie Girl Gazette*.

Brewpub menu: lunches, dinners; barbeque specials

California Condor Ale - pale ale
River Bottom Stout - dry stout
Cherokee Choice - light lager
Padres Mother Lode - lager
1989: 216 barrels
1990: N/A

(KARL STRAUSS') OLD COLUMBIA BREWERY AND GRILL
1157 Columbia Street
San Diego   92101   619-234-BREW

President: Christopher W. Cramer
Brewer: Marty Johnson
Equipment: JV Northwest

In the world of the cinema, a director might have his or her name placed above the title of a movie. But it's unusual for a brewmaster to get top billing over the name of his brewery. An exception is Karl Strauss' Old Columbia Brewery and Grill in downtown San Diego, which opened in 1989.

Strauss is a Bavarian native who learned brewing at the Technical University of Munich at Weihenstephan and served with Pabst Brewing for 44 years, retiring as vice president of production in 1983. He is a former president of the Master Brewers Association and author of *The Practical Brewer,* a widely used industry handbook.

Strauss formed Associated Microbreweries to bankroll Old Columbia and hired a cousin, Christopher Cramer, to manage it. The brewpub is located in a remodeled building and furnished with a wooden barrel vaulted ceiling, skylights, and a glass partition enabling customers to view the brewery.

Old Columbia serves three types of beer: two ales and a lager produced from recipes that Strauss brought over from the old country.

Brewpub menu: recipes made with beer including beer cheese bisque, shrimp in beer batter, and caesar salad and potato salad spiced with their beer

Gaslamp Gold - golden ale
Downtown After Dark - a dark ale
Old Columbia Lager

1989: 1,500 barrels
1990: N/A

SHIELDS BREWING
24 E. Santa Clara
Ventura 93001   805-643-1807
President/Brewer: Robert Shields
Equipment: Cross tanks

Bob and Trudy Shields built their brewery from their own resources in an industrial building in downtown Ventura that once housed a blacksmith and welding business. The town was the home of the Ventura Brewery from 1875 until Prohibition and, according to an old advertisement, sold "the Best, Coolest, and Most Delicious Beer Manufactured South of San Francisco."

Bob had been a homebrewer and electrician and Trudy a legal secretary and manager of a court reporting firm when they made the decision to open a brewpub. Bob spent a year working seven days a week to convert the building into a brewery.

Shields is Ventura County's first brewery since Prohibition. The brewpub seats 60 with 100 additional seats in the beer garden.

Brewpub menu: pubfare, appetizers, sandwiches, and beer batter and beer-steamed dinners

Gold Coast Beer - amber lager
Channel Islands Ale
Shields Stout

1989: N/A
1990: 100 barrels

SLO BREWING
1119 Garden Street
San Luis Obispo   93401   805-543-1843
President: Michael Hoffman

San Luis Obispo is on the coast halfway between San Francisco and Los Angeles. At the turn of the century, the town boasted three breweries including the McCaffrey Brothers Brewery on Garden Street.

When SLO, the city's first brewpub, was being built in 1988 in the historical Hanna Hardware Building on Garden Street, a beer bottle and tankard from the old Mc-Caffrey Brothers Brewery were uncovered. The archaeological artifacts are on display at the brewpub.

Michael Hoffman was a winemaker at HMR winery when he decided to revive Sal Luis Obispo's brewing tradition.

Brewpub menu: pubfare

Pale Ale

Amber Ale

Porter

1989: 500 barrels
1990: 845 barrels

NEW MEXICO

EMBUDO STATION/PRESTON BREWERY/SANGRE DE CRISTO BREWING
P.O. Box 156
Embudo Station 87531   505-852-4707

Co-owners: Preston & Sandy Cox
Brewer: Steve Eskeback

𝔩𝔬,𝔬𝔬𝔬 𝔣𝔬𝔬𝔱
𝔰𝔱𝔬𝔲𝔱

Embudo Station is on the Rio Grande River, 41 miles north of Sante Fe on the road to Taos. The town is a mile above sea level (5,185 ft. elevation) and has a population of 21. The original Chili Line railroad operating out of Embudo Station carried wool hides and chili out of the Rio Grande Valley before the turn of the century. Today, the area is better known for its raft trips and scenic route to Taos on State Highway 68.

In 1983, Preston and Sandy Cox discovered Embudo Station, the last 1880s-style narrow gauge New Mexico railroad station, a complex of 17 buildings listed on the National Register of Historic Places. The Coxes renovated the old smokehouse and began smoking and barbecuing meat for their Embudo Station Restaurant.

The Coxes used oak woods to create the old-fashioned smoked flavor and began attracting customers who preferred their traditional means of flavoring turkeys, rainbow trout, bacon, and hams. Although they were planning to work only during the summer tourist season, their smoked meats became so popular they started a mail order business. During the summer, tourists sit under massive cottonwood trees on the patio to enjoy the desert scenery.

The Coxes hired Steve Eskeback in 1989 to begin brewing as a subcontractor. Eskeback operates the Sangre de Cristo Brewery in the depot and produces 15 gallons a batch. He brews several exotic beer styles including a Green Chili beer that won Best of Show at the 1990 New Mexico State Fair.

Brewpub menu: New Mexico-style smoked meats, fish, barbecue

Doppelbock - *rich, dark chocolate flavored*
Weizen Ale - *brewed with wheat malt; light and crisp*
Alt - *amber ale*
Rauch - *brewed with smoked grains from their smokehouse*
10,000 Foot Stout
Mesa Pale Ale - *an India Pale Ale*
Green Chili Ale

1989: 30 barrels
1990: 100 barrels

SANTA FE BREWING
Flying M Ranch
Galisteo 87540   505-988-2340
President/Brewmaster: Mike Levis
Equipment: Used Boulder Brewery equipment

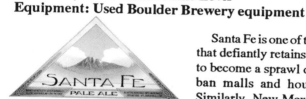

Santa Fe is one of the few Western towns that defiantly retains its charm and refuses to become a sprawl of monotonous suburban malls and housing developments. Similarly, New Mexico has developed its own art, cuisine, architecture and craft brewing tradition.

Twenty minutes from downtown Santa Fe, Mike Levis runs the Flying M Ranch outside Galisteo. He raises race horses, ropes steers, and brews beer. In the mid-1980s when he became interested in microbrewing, he purchased the original Boulder Brewery equipment after it moved into its new brewery. Boulder's Mike Lawrence installed the hardware in Levis' horse barn and helped brew his first batch in June 1987.

In one year Levis opened 116 accounts, mostly in New Mexico. Restaurants featuring New Mexican cuisine in Scottsdale, Arizona, and Northern Virginia also carry Santa Fe's Ale. Levis plans to expand the brewery's capacity to 3,000 barrels/year.

Santa Fe Pale Ale

1989: 800 barrels
1990: 550 barrels

NEVADA

UNION BREWERY
24 North C Street
Virginia City 89440   702-847-0328
Co-owners: Julie and Rick Hoover
Brewer: John Buie

Nevada finally has its first microbrewery and its first beer museum, both of which cost owners Rick and Julie Hoover only $60,000 to open. For a $2 admission fee, tourists can see the Hoovers' 600 beer cans and bottles, brewing memorabilia, and relics from the old Nevada Sierra, Tahoe, and One Sound State breweries.

The Hoovers' collection is more than the usual jumble of dusty antiques; one Fredericksburg Beer sign reportedly is worth $3,000 and old Budweiser and Coors signs are valued at $2,000. The pride of the Hoovers'collection is three cases of unopened 1944 Tahoe Beer valued at $600 a bottle! Rick Hoover learned brewing from his homebrewing father and an uncle who worked for a brewery. In 1987, he and Julie purchased the Union Brewery Saloon in historic Virginia City and began brewing one batch a week in a 1 1/2 barrel sytem. To get their state license, the Hoovers had to be in a building that had been a brewery. According to historical records, the site on North C Street housed a Union Brewery in 1865 owned by German immigrant Charles Baker after his original brewery on B Street burned down.

The Hoovers' sense of humor leans toward the bizarre -- in the downstairs museum a dried Christmas tree decorated with brassieres hangs upside down from the ceiling; mens' underwear dangle from a chandelier.

Virginia City was an 1860s gold mining town and the Union Brewery preserves the Old West flavor for tourism. Rick Hoover and brewer John Buie look like old Comstock prospectors with beards, dusty clothes, and a proud but hard-bit attitude toward their little brewery.

The saloon floor is littered with peanut shells, the walls are covered with tattered flags and flyers, and soiled dollar bills hang from the ceiling. At one time, the Union Brewery Saloon was interested only in local trade and tourists were discouraged from entering by a chair in front of the door. But today everyone is welcome to stroll though the brewery/saloon/museum for a hint of what an 1860s Virginia City saloon looked like when customers wore guns, paid bills in gold dust, and used spitoons.

Brewpub menu: pubfare

Union Brewery Beer - dark lager

1989: 200 barrels
1990: N/A

ROCKY MOUNTAINS

MICROBREWING ON THE RANGE

The rugged Rocky Mountains extend from the prairies and snow-capped mountains of Alberta, Montana, and Idaho to the deserts and wilderness of Wyoming, Colorado, and Utah. Although the area is vast and beautiful, much of it is uninhabitated or sparsely populated. But what the population lacks in numbers it makes up in character and pride that is as rugged as its wildernesses and mountains.

The microbreweries and brewpubs of the Rocky Mountains tend to reflect the gritty character of its residents who are proud of their Western heritage. The names the brewers have chosen for their microbreweries -- Wasatch, Squatters, Wynkoop, Great Northern, CooperSmith's Old Colorado, and Kessler are tied to the history of their area. Others have simply chosen geographic names for their romantic flavor: Durango, Boulder, Breckenridge, and Snake River.

The Rocky Mountains area has really only been populated for less than 150 years. And industry, in this case brewing, was never as advanced here as it was on the East or West Coasts. Agriculture, mining, and livestock have been the main industries until the energy boom after World War II. But even though the brewing tradition was not as established before Prohibition, several of the first microbreweries started in the Rocky Mountains.

ROCKY MOUNTAIN MICROBREWING PIONEERS . . .

One of the microbrewing pioneers was Boulder Brewing, which was started in 1980 in a goat shed near Hygiene, Colorado, by two professors from the University of Colorado. Tim Batt began brewing at his Snake River Brewery in Caldwell, Idaho, in 1984 on his family's hop farm. And the same year, two Helena businessmen started a microbrewery in Montana's state capital and purchased the rights to the name of a 19th century Montana Brewery: Kessler.

Boulder Brewing, one of the first Western microbreweries, started in a goat shed in Hygiene in 1979. Its new brewery in Boulder opened in 1984 and represents a contemporary architectural style that is aesthically pleasing and functional as a working brewery. The Flatiron Mountains are visible from the patio.

These three early-1980s Rocky Mountains pioneering microbreweries were similar in that all were bottling operations and were located in small towns away from urban markets (Boulder Brewery later moved to Boulder, home of the University of Colorado, and an hour's drive from Denver.) They are still operating today with only limited markets outside their region. Boulder has attempted to establish markets in select cities nationwide but has scaled back due to modest sales.

... AND MODERN ENTREPRENEURS

More recent openings of Rocky Mountains microbreweries are typical of ventures in other parts of North America -- brewpubs in suburban, urban, or university campus locations. Denver's Wynkoop, Missoula's Bayern, Salt Lake City's Squatters, and Fort Collins' CooperSmith's are contemporary brewpubs that cater to young professionals, students, and locals who have discovered the delights of freshly-brewed beer at their hometown or campus saloon.

Although bottling operations and contract breweries have opened in Sante Fe, Telluride, and Sun Valley, brewpubs seem to be the way of the future throughout the Rocky Moutains (and the rest of North America as well). Once again, microbrewing entrepreneurs see the advantage of having customers come to their establishment where competition can be limited. The riskier alternative means sending their beers out to compete against the mega-breweries' products that have a dominant place in the market supported by aggressive advertising. Of the 22 microbreweries in the Rocky Mountains states, more than half are brewpubs and three of these are co-located with bottling operations (Boulder, Bayern, and Schirf).

Liquor laws and heavy taxes in Canada do not allow the same advantages in the economic marketplace for Canadian microbrewing entrepreneurs. Alberta's three microbreweries represent the full spectrum of microbrewing from Calgary's Big Rock Brewery with numerous products and contract operations to tiny Boccalino Pasta Bistro in Edmonton.

Helena's Montana Brewery (also known as Kessler) revived the old Lorelei Beer first brewed by the state's original Kessler Brewery when Montana was a Territory. Kessler's original label was also reproduced.

Two Rocky Mountains microbreweries have taken a page from the contract brewing book that has done so well with East Coast microbrewing ventures. Kessler and Boulder have been brewing for other Western entrepreneurs and Kessler has brewed more than 30 beers for start-up operations and restaurants around the country. Both have found contract brewing to be a profitable addition to their financial ledgers.

A ROCKY MOUNTAINS BEER TREK

What an adventure to plan -- a Rocky Mountains beer trek to visit some (why not all?) of the microbreweries from Edmonton to Durango with numerous stops in between. All that is required are a few maps, plenty of gas, two weeks, and a hardy companion or two to share the adventures.

Along the way one could see the amber waves of grain in Colorado, trek along Wyoming's Teton Range, explore Montana ghost towns, visit Indian ruins in Utah, go white-river rafting in Idaho, and observe prairie dog towns in Alberta.

And then there are the Rocky Mountains microbrewed beers -- predominantly ales from brewpubs and many that have won awards and national recognition.

GREAT AMERICAN BEER FESTIVAL

A major event in the beer world is the annual Great American Beer Festival (GABF) held in Denver and hosted by the Boulder-based Institute of Brewing Studies and its companion organization, the American Homebrewers Association. AHA has been a leader in representing the microbrewing industry in North America and furthering the popular homebrewing movement.

Every year the GABF attracts thousands of beer lovers, tourists, aspiring microbrewers, and the curious who want to sample a selection of the hundreds of beers collected for the festival. In 1990, 3,000 people sampled 400 beers from 140 breweries the first weekend in November. A professional judging panel awarded gold, silver, and bronze medals in 10 ale categories, 14 lager categories, and 7 hybrid categories (see Chapter 1, "The State of the Industry: Microbrewing in the 1990s").

But the GABF is more than just sampling exotic beers and handing out medals; it's a rare opportunity to meet the leaders in the industry from all over North America and to hear how and why they became craft brewers.

If you are interested in attending the GABF, call AHA (303-447- 0816) for the date and location of the next festival.

ALBERTA

BIG ROCK BREWERY
6403 35 Street, SE
Calgary   T2C 1N2   403-279-2917

President: Ed McNally
Brewer: Bernd Pieper

Ed McNally started the Big Rock Brewery in 1985 and hired German brewmaster Bernd Pieper to design several beers including Canadian-style lagers, English-style ales, and Scottish-style porters.

Big Rock also brews house brands for Alberta restaurants and deluxe hotels in nearby Chateau Lake Louise and Banff Springs Hotel in the Canadian Rockies.

Big Rock brews with two-row Canadian malting barley and Yakima hops. Big Rock's unpasteurized beers are sold from Inuvik on the Arctic Ocean to San Diego.

Pale Ale
Traditional Ale
Bitter
Cock O' the Rock Porter
McNally's Extra
XO Lager
Royal Coachman Dry Ale

BOCCALINO PASTA BISTRO
10525 Jasper Avenue
Edmonton TJ5 1Z4   403-462-7313
President: Nanci-Lee Burrows

STRATHCONA BREWING
4914-A 89th Street
Edmonton T6E 5K1   403-465-0553
President: Don Moore

COLORADO

ASPEN BEER COMPANY
P.O. Box 4923
Aspen   81612   303-923-6505
President: Charles Bontempo
Equipment: Contract brewery

The formulation for Aspen's beer was an after-hours venture by the four partners who are all avid skiers and work in Aspen/Snowmass restaurants. Their beer is brewed at Boulder Brewing. If the contract brewing venture is successful, the partners would like to open a brewpub in the Aspen area.

Aspen Silver City Ale - brewed with Colorado pale malt and 100% Hallerauer hops
1989: 200 barrels
1990: N/A

BOULDER BREWING
2880 Wilderness Place
Boulder 80301   303-444-8448
President: Mike Lawrence

Boulder is one of the first microbreweries founded in North America. David Hummer and "Stick" Ware were University of Colorado professors in 1979 when they started their brewing venture in a goatshed near Hygiene.

After their initial flourish of success, they raised $3 million from investors and moved in 1984 into an impressive cathedral-like building in Boulder. Their new location is in an industrial park south of town that allows a view of the Flatirons mountains which are on their labels. The brewery's twin silos hold the grain which is fed by gravity into the brew kettle on the ground level.

The attractive design of the Boulder Brewery allows visitors to see the brew kettle at the entrance, watch the bottling assembly in the glass-enclosed hospitality room, and later have lunch on the outdoor patio. This is certainly one of the most spectacular microbreweries in North America.

Boulder's ales are brewed with Colorado two-row malt, Cascade and Halleratau hops, and water from the Arapahoe Glacier. Their beers have regularly won awards in local and national festivals.

Boulder Pale Ale
Boulder Porter
Boulder Stout

1989: 3,798 barrels
1990: 3,384 barrels

BRECKENRIDGE BREWING
600 South Main
Breckenridge   80424   303-453-1550
Co-owners: Richard Squire, Tim Lenahan

CARVERS BREWING
1022 Main Street
Durango   81301   303-259-2545
President: Bill Carver
Equipment: Continental Breweries and used equipment

Bill Carver opened his brewpub in the family's bakery restaurant in the picturesque southwestern Colorado town of Durango, which once was home to 13 breweries. Some of Carver's brewing equipment belonged to Milwaukee's Century Hall Brewery which was destroyed by a fire.

Carver was attracted to the idea of opening a brewpub because brewing beer and baking bread require similar ingredients. He brews seasonal beers including raspberry ale, cherry stout, ginger beer, and root beer (5% alcohol). Carver says his biggest reward is seeing customers smile when they try his beers.

Brewpub menu: sandwiches, soups, salads, entrees

Purgatory Honey Pilsener - brewed with pale and crystal malts and honey
Animas City Amber Ale - English-style ale
Iron Horse Stout - medium-bodied stout.

1989: 400 barrels
1990: 450 barrels

COOPERSMITH'S PUB AND BREWERY
#5 Old Town Square
Ft. Collins   80524   303-498-0483

President: Scott Smith
Brewer: Brad Page

The name CooperSmith's is doubly significant. Cooper Smith happens to be the name of owner Scott Smith's year-old son who is a few years away from his first legal beer. Cooper also means barrelmaker -- a trade that was of critical importance to early breweries. Abraham Lincoln's father and John F. Kennedy's great- grandfather once practiced this noble craft.

CooperSmith's opened in 1989 and is a joint venture with Denver's Wynkoop Brewery. Smith brought his skills as restaurateur to the operation; brewer Brad Page trained at Wynkoop while CooperSmith's was under construction.

Despite 60-hour work weeks and profit margins averaging a mere 5%, Smith would like to open more brewpubs -- sort of a "foam on the range" approach. "It's like having a party at your house every night," he confesses.

Brewpub menu: Southwest specialties such as green chili stew, mesa bean cakes, creole catfish gumbo, and a veggie pot pie

Pedestrian Ale - light ale
Poudre Pale Ale - light bodied, with a reddish color from the addition of crystal malt
Albert Damm Bitter - heavier, more highly-hopped ale; named after a baker who once occupied the brewery site
Horsetooth Stout
Nut Brown Ale
Linden Light Lager

1989: 195 barrels
1990: 1,100 barrels

DURANGO BREWING
3000 Main Avenue
Durango 81301   303-247-3396

Co-owners: Steven & Linda McClaren
Brewer: Steven McClaren

Steve McClaren was a custom bike maker and ski instructor when he and his wife began planning their own brewery in Durango in the Four Corners region of southwestern Colorado. They visited breweries in Europe, Australia, and the West Coast and liked German beer styles the most.

The McClarens began brewing in April 1990; their Durango Dark Lager won a Bronze medal at the 1990 Great American Beer Festival. Durango's six-barrel brewhouse has a capacity of 600 barrels/year which they sell mostly to local accounts.

Durango Dark Lager
1990: 150 barrels

HUBCAP BREWERY & KITCHEN
143 East Meadow Drive
Vail   81657   303-476-5757

President/Brewer: Wayne Wannanen

Hubcap is Colorado's newest brewpub, opening in January 1991 in Vail's Crossroads Shopping Center. The name derives from hubcaps decorating the walls of the brewpub.

Brewpub menu: home-cooked food

White River Wheat
Camp Hale Golden Ale
Ace Amber Ale
Beaver Tail Pale Ale
Rainbow Trout Stout

ODELL BREWING
119 Lincoln Avenue
Fort Collins   80524   303-498-9070
President/Brewer: Doug Odell

Colorado is becoming a hotbed of the Western microbrewing industry. The mega-breweries of Anheuser-Busch and Coors supply the volume, while the state's dozen microbreweries provide the variety and charm. Fort Collins, a college town of about 65,000, has three microbreweries of its own.

Odell Brewing is a family-owned operation that turned out its first keg in November 1989. Owner and brewmaster Doug Odell is a veteran homebrewer who served an apprenticeship at Anchor and studied at UC-Davis. His brewery is in a converted grain elevator built in 1915.

Odell brews three top-fermented beers: a brown ale, a bitter, and a wheat beer. After less than a year in operation, Odell received a blessing when beer writer Michael Jackson visited the brewery and pronounced Odell's 90 Shilling Ale the best of the local beers.

90 Shilling Ale - malty, full-bodied brown ale, brewed with Northern Brewer and Cascade hops
Heartland Wheat Ale - described by Jackson as "relatively light, very dry, an extremely refreshing beer;" made from 45% wheat malt and a blend of Cascade, Tettnang, and Saaz hops
Old Town Ale - copper-colored bitter ale

1989: 32 barrels
1990: 897 barrels

OLD COLORADO BREWING
180 N. College
Ft. Collins   80524   303-493-2739
Co-owners: Joe and Marilyn Neckel, Tom and Carrie Rulon
Brewers: Al Colby, Jim Whitmer, Jim Neckel, Tom Rulon

The four homebrewers who founded Old Colorado claim to have a combined 160 years brewing experience. One of the founders, Al Colby, also sold home brewing equipment and supplies in Ft. Collins.

The brewpub opened in July 1989 in the historical Northern Hotel a few blocks from the campus of Colorado State University. Two seasonal beers brewed are Old Colorado Rauch and Continental Divide Bitter Ale; other seasonals are brewed at Christmas, the Fourth of July, and Octoberfest.

Brewpub menu: pubfare

Fort Collins Pride - pale amber ale
Long's Peak Pilsener
Prouder Porter

1989: 133 barrels
1990: 189 barrels

TELLURIDE BREWING
P.O. Box 819
Telluride   81435   801-259-6008
President: Steve Patterson
Equipment: Contract brewer with Huber

Steve Patterson, a former electrical engineer, accountant, and professional speed skier, became enchanted with microbrewing while living in the resort town of Telluride. He wanted to start a microbrewery but the population of Telluride is small and seasonal, so Patterson started contract brewing with Huber in Wisconsin in 1987.

Telluride Beer has won awards at the Great American Beer Festival. Telluride is distributed in 17 states, principally in the West. Although Patterson moved to Utah to open a brewpub, he still plans to build a microbrewery in Telluride.

Telluride Beer - American lager brewed with four malts and four hops
1989: 1,368 barrels
1990: 1,500 barrels

WALNUT BREWING
1123 Walnut
Boulder 80302   303-447-1345
President: Mark Youngquist

WYNKOOP BREWERY
1634 18th Street
Denver 80202   303-297-2700
Co-owners: John Hickenlooper and Jerry Williams
Brewer: Russ Schehrer
Equipment: Newlands

Colorado's first brewpub and Denver's first brewery in 50 years, Wynkoop takes its name from Edward Wanshear Wynkoop, a frontier fort commander, sheriff, and amateur actor who was one of the city's founding fathers. Wynkoop was unpopular in his time; he believed in peaceful coexistence with the local Cheyenne and Arapahoe tribes when most settlers believed that the only good Indian was a dead one.

Wynkoop Brewing, however, has enjoyed uniformly good press since opening in October 1988. The *Denver Post* counted it among "the 25 best reasons to live in Denver." The brewpub was founded by John Hickenlooper and Jerry Williams, a pair of unemployed geologists who hooked up with award-winning homebrewer Russ Schehrer and chef Mark Schiffler. Schehrer was American Homebrewers Association Homebrewer of the Year in 1985.

The four Denver entrepreneurs raised $600,000 and located Wynkoop a block from Union Station in the 90-year old Brown Mercantile building which is on the National Register of Historic Places. Much of the original decor -- arched windows, oak paneling and tin ceilings -- has been preserved. An outdoor terrace, flowerboxes, and a black concrete bar were added to the old West architectural motif.

Brewmaster Schehrer's brewing portfolio includes 20 different recipes with 6 on tap at any given time. His specialties include Splatz Porter, Quinn's Scottish Ale, O'Kerry's Irish Stout, and Hickenlooper Light. Schehrer says every Englishman in Denver comes by when he brews his Extra Special Bitter to get their fix.

Wynkoop features a private dining room, a beer garden, a bar which features 15 single malt scotches, and a Jazz Works club for music lovers. The partners and their investors opened a second brewpub, CooperSmith's, in Fort Collins.

Brewpub menu: American pubfare with specialties using ingredients from brewing: raw barley used in baking barley rolls, malt to make chocolate malted mousse, and sausage dishes cooked with beer.

Wilderness Wheat - used in the house specialty Gorgonzola Ale soup; Wynkoop's variation on the traditional beer cheese soup

St. Charles ESB

India Pale Ale

Sagebrush Stout

1989: 1,300 barrels
1990: 1,814 barrels

IDAHO

COEUR D'ALENE BREWING/T.W. FISHER'S BREWPUB
204 North Second Street
Coeur d'Alene 83814   208-664-2739
President: Tom Fisher
Equipment: Custom fabricated

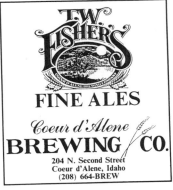

T. W. Fisher's was Idaho's first brewpub when it opened in July 1987 and began brewing in November. The brewery doubled production within six months and again in 1989.

The brewpub (still the only one in Idaho) is located on a corner one block from main street and a short walk from scenic Lake Coeur d'Alene. The area is noted for its summer and winter sports activities including hunting, fishing, skiing, boating and camping. Fisher's theme is contemporary saloon with brewery coasters and platters decorating the walls. The brewery is undergoing expansion at the rear of the building.

Distribution of Fisher's beers has expanded throughout Idaho and into neighboring Washington, Oregon, and Montana.

Brewpub menu: pubfare and pizza

Centennial Pale Ale
Festival Dark
Weizen Light
Full Moon Stout
1989: 1,605 barrels
1990: N/A

SNAKE RIVER BREWING
16412 Willis Road
Caldwell 83605   208-459-7234

President: Tim Batt
Brewmaster: Hoe Arrendondo
Equipment: Locally-manufactured, Italian bottling line

Tim Batt started one of America's first microbreweries when he opened Snake River in June 1983 and sold his first beer in September 1984. His amber lager won third place in the consumer preference poll at the 1985 GABF.

The Batt family raises hops on their farm and the brewery is located in the middle of a hop field. Distribution of Snake River Amber Lager is limited to Boise Valley and Seattle.

Snake River Amber Lager
1989: 535 barrels
1990: N/A

SUN VALLEY BREWING
201 North Main Street
Sun Valley 83353   208-788-5777

President/Brewer: Gordon M. Gammell
Equipment: Contract brewed at Kessler

Describing himself as a skiing geologist who abandoned the earth sciences "to scrub dirty tanks in the thankless world of microbrewing," Gordon M. Gammell hooked up with partner Michael Kraynick to found Sun Valley Brewing in 1986. They began as contract brewers, renting the facilities of Kessler Brewing in Montana until they raised money to build their own plant.

Eventually, Gammell wants to expand to a capacity of 2-3,000 barrels/year and open a brewpub. Sun Valley won a gold and two silver medals at the 1989 GABF and a gold and bronze in 1990.

Sun Valley White Cloud Ale - *silver medal winner in alt category at 1989 GABF*

Sun Valley Sawtooth Gold Lager - *golden pilsener*

Sun Valley Holiday Ale - *gold medal winner at 1989 and 1990 GABF for Scottish-style ale*

Sun Valley Blonde - *bronze medal winner in blond/golden ale category at 1990 GABF*

Cabin Fever Barleywine

1989: 1,000 barrels
1990: N/A

MONTANA

BAYERN BREWING
North Higgins and Railroad
Missoula 59807-8043   406-721-8705

President: Reinhard Schulte
Brewer: Jurgen Knoller

Bayern Brewing, which opened in 1987, is in a depot of the defunct Northern Pacific Railroad, a turn-of-the-century red brick building listed in the National Register of Historic Places. The railroad brewpub is the creation of German businessman Reinhard Schulte who divides his time between Lake Constance in Bavaria where he works as as tax consultant to German breweries and his Valley of the Moon ranch outside Missoula.

Bayern was designed by Dan Carey, a brewing consultant who also built Helena's Kessler Brewery. The brewery equipment is behind glass at the front of the depot.

Montana has not legalized brewpubs so the restaurant is run as a separate business by Eric Newman and Ray Risho. The restaurant buys 80% of Bayern's beers and serves them in the bar, restaurant, and beer garden.

Bayern is the German name for Bavaria, the homeland of brewer Jurgen Knoller, who serves kegs the old-fashioned way, by pounding a brass spigot through the bung of a wooden keg. Bayern's beers are sold in five-liter kegs; special orders for 28-gallon wooden barrels are sold for $300.

Brewpub menu: pubfare, with Mediterranean specialties

Bayern Pilsener - *golden lager brewed with two-row Klages malt, Saaz and Hallertau hops*
Bayern Amber - *a Marzen-style beer*
1989: 1,100 barrels
1990: 1,100 barrels

GREAT NORTHERN BREWING
P.O. Box 1386
Columbia Falls   59912   406-862-0704

Co-owners: Louis and Sheryl Van Duzer

Columbia Falls is a stop on the Great Northern railroad in Montana's Rocky Mountains 30 miles from the entrance to Glacier National Park. Fishing,

hunting, camping, skiing, and mountain climbing are a few of the attractions that draw tourists and outdoorsmen to one of Montana's most beautiful corners.

The Van Duzers operate their little 2-barrel brewery by themselves and sell to about 20 accounts around the Flathead Valley. Great Northern's label is a scenic view of the Rocky Mountains in autumn.

Great Northern Lager
1989: N/A
1990: N/A

MONTANA BEVERAGE, LTD (KESSLER BREWING)
1439 Harris Street
Helena   59601   406-449-6214

President: Bruce DeRosier
Brewer: Steve Schellhardt
Equipment: Combination of old dairy equipment and locally-manufactured tanks

Nicholas Kessler opened a brewery in the Montana Territory in the 19th century and the name was closely tied to early Montana history. Bruce DeRosier purchased rights to the name before he opened his Helena microbrewery in 1983.

Kessler Brewing is located in Helena, the capital of Montana, a state which borders on two other sparsely populated states, Idaho and Wyoming. So to survive in a small market, Kessler brews more than 20 contract beers for microbreweries and restaurants around the country.

Kessler's beers have won national awards at festivals and tastings around the country, including the Great American Beer Festival. Kessler Bock has been rated as one of the best bocks brewed in the world. In 1989, Kessler began exporting beer to Japan where it reportedly sold for $5 a bottle in a department store chain.

During Montana's Centennial in 1989, Kessler brewed Centennial Beer as the state's official beer and sold in long neck bottles packed in wooden cases. DeRosier says the Centennial recipe was similar to the original beer brewed by Nicholas Kessler in Helena in 1865. Kessler plans to expand to 10,000 barrels/year and to open a brewpub.

Kessler's colorful label for its Lorelei Beer is a reproduction of the turn-of-the-century label showing a wispy maiden beckoning to a sailer in a moody, gothic setting.

Kessler Lager - *amber-colored, malty texture*

Kessler Wheat - *slightly dark, hoppy, refreshing effervescence*

Kessler Oktoberfest - *brewed with blend of pale and dark malts and Saaz hops to produce rich, amber-colored lager*

Kessler Bock - *brewed with two-row Klages malt, caramel and black and a blend of Cascades, Bullion, and Hersbrucker hops; highly rated*

Lorelei Extra Pale - *crisp, pale lager*

1989: 3,600 barrels
1990: N/A

UTAH

EDDIE MC STIFF'S
57 South Main
Moab   84532   801-259-6008
Co-Owners: Steve Patterson, Ed Snyder, Mike McTigue
Equipment: Newlands

Eddie McStiff's is scheduled to open in the Spring of 1991 on the Colorado River in the foothills of the La Sal mountains. The area is an oasis in the middle of the Utah desert once known for its mining. Now it is a popular stop for river rafters and mountain bikers.

The 220-seat brewpub is in a 7,000 sq. ft. building with a Victorian facade. A patio and beer garden will open in the summer. A non-alcoholic beer will be brewed in addition to four beers on tap. Co-owner Steve Patterson founded Telluride Brewery, a contract microbrewery in Colorado in 1987.

Brewpub menu: New York-style pizzas, pasta, pubfare

SALT LAKE BREWING/SQUATTER'S PUB BREWERY
147 West Broadway
Salt Lake City   84101   801-363-2739
President: Jeff Polychronis

Owner Jeff Polychronis is counting on there being enough lovers of real ale to support a brewpub in Utah, a state known for being dry. Squatter's is located in downtown Salt Lake City not far from the symphony hall, hotels, and arena where the Utah Jazz NBA team plays.

Squatter's opened in 1989 in a turn-of-the-century building that once served as a rooming house for railroad workers, newspaper reporters, laborers, and transients. Known as the Boston Hotel, it was operated by a Latvian immigrant named Ethel Yudin who rented rooms for 35 to 50 cents a night. Working men liked it because it was near the Rio Grande depot where railroad crews were hired. Nearby were saloons which sold nickel schooners with free lunch. The years hadn't treated the structure kindly before Jeff Polychronis and Peter Cole leased it for their brewpub.

Prior to becoming a brewpub, the building was the Jazz Ranch. Polychronis had to repaint the exterior which had been daubed flourescent orange-pink. To support the weight of brewing equipment, he buttressed the interior with timbers from a bridge to the Anadonda mine near Tooele. An urban renewal project provided cobblestones for building a hearth in the pub.

Squatter's serves three ales and specials including a wheat beer, porter, nut brown, and a pilsener.

Brewpub menu: pubfare, pizzas

City Creek Pale Ale - *brewed with pale malt, Clusters and Willamette hops*
Emigration Amber Ale - *well-balanced, copper-colored brew made with pale and caramel malts, Cascade and Chinook hops*
Millcreek Cream Stout - *full-bodied, Irish stout brewed with pale, caramel, chocolate malt, and Chinook hops*
1989: 320 barrels
1990: 1,150 barrels

SCHIRF BREWING/WASATCH BREW PUB
250 Main Street
Park City 84060   801-645-9500
President: Greg Schirf
Brewer: Mellie Pullman
Equipment: 17 -barrel copper kettle custom built by coppersmith Paul Zaft

Utah would seem to be a singularly unpromising spot to start a brewery. Sixty percent of the population abstains for religious reasons, and the state beer tax of $11 per barrel is the highest in the West.

Greg Schirf hasn't done badly, all things considered. In 1986 he opened the state's first independent brewery since the Becker Brewery in Ogden shut down in 1965. Demand for his beer forced Schirf to double production his first two years in business. In 1988, he successfully petitioned the state legislature to make brewpubs legal. The next year he built the 14,000 square foot building that now houses his brewing and bottling works, three bars, and a full-service restaurant.

Wasatch Brewpub takes its name from a local mountain range. Schirf grew up in Milwaukee where both his grandfathers made homebrew during Prohibition. He flirted with the idea of opening a brewery but didn't act until he met his future brewmaster, Mellie Pullman, on a ski trip. She was a homebrewer herself and a descendant of the founder of Schlitz Brewing.

Pullman brews a lager, ale, wheat beer and stout as well as seasonal beers. All are unpasteurized and follow the Reinheitsgebot Purity Law. The Schirf Brewery isn't out to make a fortune: "We drink our share and sell the rest," is Greg's motto. He credits his mother with helping him choose his vocation: "She told me that making beer was a recession-proof occupation because during bad times people drink to forget and during good times they drink to celebrate."

Brewpub menu: pubfare and entrees with a Mexican or Cajun accent

Wasatch Ale - a dark amber, aromatic ale brewed with four types of Yakima hops and a special strain of yeast; voted one of the top ten beers at the 1988 Great American Beer Festival

Slickrock Lager - light lager brewed with a blend of Saaz, Tettnanger and Yakima hops and aged 45 days

Wasatch Gold - mildly hopped German-style wheat beer complemented by a slice of lime or lemon

Irish Stout - lighter than a Guinness, this traditional stout is brewed with five types of malted barleys

1989: 2,700 barrels
1990: 2,700 barrels

WYOMING

OTTO BROTHERS' BREWING
P.O. Box 4177
Jackson   83001   307-733-9000
President/Brewer: Charlie Otto
Equipment: JV Northwest, used dairy tanks

Charlie Otto doesn't mind commuting to work every morning; the Otto Brothers Brewery, which he built himself, is located in his backyard. Charlie and his brother Ernie hatched the idea of starting a microbrewery after years of homebrewing and trips to Germany and Austria, the land of their ancestors. When Otto Brothers' Brewery opened in 1989, it became Wyoming's first brewery in 125 years.

Otto Brothers produces three varieties of cask-conditioned ales and plans to brew a weizen. Their beers are available only around Teton County where they're sold at such well-known outlets as the Mangy Moose, the Calico Pizza Parlor, Spirits of the West, and the Million Dollar Cowboy Bar.

Charlie and Ernie are former geologists who fell in love with mountaineering and outdoor sports. They're doing their part for environmental consciousness by selling their beer in 64 oz. reuseable bottles called "growlers." "Throwaway containers represent about 40% of the price you pay for consumable products," says Ernie.

Teton Ale - *copper-colored, English-style ale brewed with Cascade and Chinook hops*

Moose Juice Stout - *brewed with several dark malts with chocolate being predominate; served with Teton Ale and called a "black and tan"*

Teton Pale Ale - *light ale developed for summer drinking*

1989: 99 barrels
1990: 206 barrels

THE PACIFIC RIM

MICROBREWING IN THE TROPICS AND THE ARCTIC

Tropical Hawaii and snow-covered Alaska would seem to be the alpha and omega of vacationlands. Hawaii seduces with sun-washed beaches and year-around balmy weather; Alaska calls to the adventurer seeking the splendor and danger of North America's last great wilderness. Both states have a common brewing tradition established by the pioneers who settled these far-flung outposts and sought a life better than what they had left.

Alaska and Hawaii originally were peopled by aboriginal tribes with rich traditions that are still romanticized today. Alaska was first settled by neighboring Russian explorers seeking new frontiers and the wealth of furbearing animals. Hawaii was discovered by Europeans searching for a tropical paradise flowing with milk and honey. Centuries later, those dreams are still powerful attractions for the adventurous as well as the world weary.

Alaska's first brewery was built by the Russian governor in 1865, four doors down from his residence in Sitka. That plant turned out *kvass,* a low-alcohol, uncarbonated beverage made from fermented bread. Under American rule, the Land of the

Midnight Sun has had 38 breweries -- many short-lived operations during the Gold Rush days of the early twentieth century.

Following Prohibition, seven breweries sprang up in Hawaii
manufacturing beer and sake, the traditional Japanese rice wine
which, since it is made from fermented grain, is technically a beer.
The most successful brewery, Honolulu's Hawaii Brewing,
lasted until 1979. It spent its last years as a subsidiary of Joseph
Schlitz until the company decided it was cheaper to brew the local
Primo brand in Los Angeles and ship it to Hawaii. Primo is still
made by Stroh, but it no longer enjoys the two-thirds share of the
Hawaiian market that it reached in the 1960s.

TO QUENCH A THIRST OR FEED A HUNGER

The microbrewery revolution came to both Alaska and Hawaii
in 1986. As might be expected, the types of beers brewed by the
microbreweries were determined by the climate. Since Hawaii is
a warm weather paradise, the beers of choice are light and
thirst-quenching pale pilseners. With the exception of Koolau
Lager, a European-style pilsener, Hawaii's local brews are variations of the light and slightly bitter mainstream beers from the
continent. "We didn't want to knock anybody out in this climate,"
explained Aloysius Klink, president of Pacific Brewing.

Alaskan Brewing's Geoff Larson, on the other hand, would
have little use for a light beer. His customers, who include miners,
trappers, and pipeline workers, drink beer not only to relax but
for its food value. One needs a storehouse of extra calories to burn
off during long arctic winters. Alaskan Brewing's beers are not
only stouter in character, but come with distinctive tastes that
could be matched as well with moose steaks or bear stew as they
would with tamer roasts in the lower 48. One doesn't come to
Alaska, after all, to have what the boys in Peoria are having.

ICEBERGS, AVALANCHES, AND MILES OF OCEAN

Brewing in the Pacific Rim, however, is cursed by geography. The remoteness of these breweries creates problems with transportation of both supplies and the finished product. Hops, barley, and brewing equipment have to be shipped thousands of miles over rough seas to reach their destination. That takes time and, more importantly, money for the long-distance ocean-going travel.

Fortunately, both Hawaii and Alaska have excellent local sources of water. But with this one small advantage, the Pacific breweries must cope with greater problems if they ship beer to distant markets. Broken bottles, long and rugged travel with a perishable product, spoiled beer, and temperature extremes are problems that would cause any well-meaning (and well-funded) microbrewer to think twice before expanding distribution to continental markets.

Larson in particular faces formidable obstacles; Juneau is cut off from the highway system by water and ice, forcing him to ship his beer via boat and airplane. It's also "one of the most avalanche-prone cities in America," he explains, with the nearby Mendenhall Glacier and extensive ice fields. "We had six avalanches in 1989, one of which knocked out the power plant. Five back-up generators went out of order within 12 hours. They divided Juneau into four sectors and had rotating blackouts."

Although Pacific Rim microbreweries will rise or fall depending on their success with local markets, they ship some of their output to the continental United States. But expect to pay a premium; during a Christmas time 1989 visit to Washington, DC, Larson brought along a shipment of 12 oz. bottles, which wound up retailing at a local liquor outlet for about $5 a bottle!

Brewing in the Pacific Rim states also poses problems that other microbreweries do not face. Foremost is the limited market.

Geoff Larson and his wife Marcy bottling their Alaskan Amber, winner of Best Beer in America at the Great American Beer Festival in 1988.

Neither Alaska nor Hawaii has a major urban population like Seattle, Denver, or San Francisco to support a microbrewery capable of brewing a respectable 10,000 barrels a year. Neither are there neighboring states with urban centers to develop a regional market. A microbrewery in Alaska or Hawaii can saturate the local market but face high costs to support expansion. For those reasons, the prospect for more bottling microbreweries looks limited in Alaska and Hawaii. And until state legislatures legalize brewpubs, microbrewing appears to have limited potential for future ventures.

Look for another entry or two from the Pacific states, but not the blossoming as in other Western states.

ALASKA

ALASKAN BREWING
5429 Shaune Drive
Douglas   99824   907-780-5866
President/Brewer: Geoff Larson

A word of caution to tourists planning to visit the Alaskan Brewery -- you can't drive there from the lower 48. Alaska's capital, Juneau, is accessible only by air or sea . . . and sometimes not even then because of nasty weather or landslides.

Despite the obvious distribution problems this creates, Geoff Larson sells his entire output within the state (with occasional shipments to Japan). A chemical engineer by education, Larson installed alcohol processing plants in the Midwest and worked at a gold mine before turning his homebrewing hobby into a profession. His wife Marcy is a partner in the operation.

Alaska, by Larson's reckoning, was home to 48 breweries before Prohibition. None were light beer producers: "Alaskans have always needed a higher caloric content," Larson says, "so they want food value in their beer."

Alaskan's original flagship brand was Chinook Alaskan Amber, Chinook being a term with regional appeal: it refers to an Indian tribe, a southwesterly wind, and a salmon. Larson dropped the name because of its potential for confusion--Chinook is also the name of a hop and a Washington winery.

Larson taps a local glacier for his brewery's water supply that's soft and free of vegetable matter. "We pre-age our water 10,000 years," Larson laughs. In 1988, Alaskan Amber was voted Best Beer in America at the Great American Beer Festival after Samuel Adams had won the title for three straight years. Larson also brews a unique smoked porter as a holiday beer.

Alaskan Amber - full-bodied, malty taste with Saaz hops; an alt-style beer based on a 1907 recipe from the original Douglas Brewery; winner of gold medal in alt class in 1987-88, and 1990 at the GABF and Best Beer in America in 1988

Alaskan Pale Ale - brewed with a blend of Chinook, Tettnang, and Willamette hops and dry-hopped to give it a fragrant, flowery aroma and fruity taste

Alaskan Smoked Porter - brewed with four malt varieties and two strains of hops; silver medalist at 1987 and 1990 GABF

Alaska Autumn Ale - copper-colored, full bodied ale with crisp, hoppy taste and pine-like spicey overtone; silver medal winner at the 1990 GABF

1989: 4,000 barrels
1990: 4,200 barrels

YUKON BREWING
7851 Spring Street
Anchorage 99518 907-349-7191
President/Brewer: Adolf Zeman
Equipment: Stainless steel tanks and fermenters manufactured locally; bottler and labeller from Germany

Well-traveled is the word for Adolf Zeman, founder of the Yukon Brewery. He was born in Medlesice, Czechoslovakia, where his father ran a brewery. As a young man he worked in Germany's famous Hofbrauhaus, then returned to his homeland after World War II to earn his degree as brewmaster.

In 1948 Zeman fled Czechoslovakia and wound up as a brewer in Tehran. The capital of Iran is now officially dry under Islamic fundamentalist rule, but then it had three breweries. He worked there for eight years, then plied his trade in Argentina.

Zeman came to Alaska in 1968 when the state had no indigenous breweries. He worked in the plumbing, heating, and construction businesses until 1989 when he put together a group of 18 shareholders to finance a microbrewery. Yukon turned out its first beer in bottles in February 1991.

Arctic Gold - a pilsener brewed from a mixture of American, German and Czech hops
1990: N/A

HAWAII

HONOLULU BREWING
411 Puuhale Road
Honolulu   96819-3240   808-845-5050

President: Klaus O. Haberich
Brewer: Hans G. Kestler
Equipment: Used and new equipment from Germany, France, and U.S.

Most immigrants to Hawaii are lured by the year-around warmth and the prospect of living in a lush tropical paradise. Hans Kestler and Klaus Haberich were lured by the lucrative beer market. Hawaii ranks fifth in the nation for per capita beer consumption, equivalent to a six-pack a week for every inhabitant. Haberich will be happy to capture 5% of that market.

Honolulu Brewing is located in an industrial sector of the city near the state prison. It started as the Koolau Brewery in 1988 but was acquired by a New Zealand firm, Wilson Neill of Dunedin, after a slow start. The new owner acquired majority ownership and infused the company with capital, changed the name, and expanded the product line.

Brewmaster Kestler's grandfather owned a brewery in Ansbach, Germany. His father toiled as brewmaster for the Maisel Brewery and Kestler himself has been in the trade since he was 14. Before coming to Hawaii, he served as chief of the Blatz microbrewery in Milwaukee, Heileman's brief experiment with specialty brewing.

Honolulu's new owners have ambitious plans. They intend to expand capacity from 10,000 to 40,000 barrels a year, start exporting beer to Japan and the continental U.S. markets, and introduce ales and seasonal beers.

Koolau Lager - *a well-hopped European-style pilsener brewed with two-row Canadian malted barley; named after a mountain range on Oahu*

Koolau Light - *a less bitter version of Koolau Lager with one-third fewer calories and a reduced alcoholic content*

Diamond Head Dry - *more highly fermented to achieve a crisp finish with no aftertaste; silver medal winner at the 1989 GABF.*

Pali Hawaiian Beer - *standard domestic lager; brewed with California rice added to the barley malt*

1989: 2,000 barrels
1990: 5,300 barrels

PACIFIC BREWING
Imi Kala Street
Wailuku, Maui 96793   808-244-0396
President: Al Klink
Brewer: Gunter Dittrich

Pacific Brewing had its genesis in 1982 when real estate developer Aloysius Klink sent his son Michael to study in Germany. Michael wound up working at a family-owned brewery in Traunstein, Bavaria. The owners eventually became friends of the elder Klink and convinced him there was a market in Hawaii for a locally brewed European-style beer.

Klink didn't get the ball rolling until he met Klaus Haberich, a university professor, in 1984. Haberich had been unsuccessfully trying to bankroll a regional brewery with a 50,000 barrels-a-year capacity. The two expatriate Berliners incorporated in 1985 and raised $2.5 million to build a more modest facility. The brewery occupies an old sugar mill on the northern side of the island of Maui. It produces bottled beer only -- about 3,500 cases a week.

Brewmaster Gunter Dittrich was hired to oversee production. The equipment, hops, malt, and yeast are all imported from Europe. Only the water is local: rainwater filtered through lava from the nearby West Maui Mountains. At one time Maui Lager was exported to the continental United States and available as far away as Washington, DC. The brewery discontinued shipments because of legal and financial problems. Pacific is currently suing its former mainland distributor for breech of contract, alleging that the distributor failed to purchase an agreed-upon allotment of 6,500 cases per month.

Pacific Brewing claims that it suffered severe losses and was forced to sell its property and enter into a 10-year leaseback agreement. Haberich has left the company to become president of the rival Honolulu Brewing; Klink still serves as president. Currently he's trying to find a contract brewer on the mainland to can his beer for the Hawaiian airline market. He also wants to reestablish sales on the mainland.

Maui Lager - *brewed with imported 2-row malt and Hallertau hops, but lighter and less bitter than a European pilsener to suit local tastes*

Maui Lager Light - *contains one-third fewer calories than the regular Maui Lager*

1989: 2,000 barrels
1990: N/A

INDEX

A

Alaskan Brewing 196, 197
All About Beer 1, 6, 28
Alpine Village Hofbrau 148
American Brewer 1, 6, 13, 28, 39, 44
American Homebrewers Association 21, 22, 28
Anchor Brewing 3, 14, 15, 33, 36, 41, 42
Anderson Valley Brewing 64
Angeles Brewing 148
Anheuser-Busch 10
Aspen Beer Company 175

B

Back Alley Brewery 65
Bandersnatch Brewpub 143
Barley's Brewpub 144
Bayern Brewing 186
Bay Front Brewery 127
Beer Institute 2
Belmont Brewing 149
Big Rock Brewery 173
Big Time Brewery 108
Bison Brewery 42
Boccalino Pasta Bistro 174
Boulder Brewery 168, 175
Boulder Creek Brewing 43
B. Moloch's/The Heathman Bakery 125
Breckenridge Brewing 176
Brewhouse Grill/State Street Brewing 149
Brewpub on the Green 43
Bridgeport Brewpub 127, 128
Brown Street Brewery 55
Buckerfield's Brewery 93
Buffalo Bill's Brewpub 3, 18, 36, 44
Butterfield Brewing 150

C

Callahan's Pub 151

California Celebrator 2, 6, 29, 38, 39
CAMRA (Campaign for Real Ale) 83, 106
Carvers Brewing 176
Cascade Beer News 2, 6, 23, 29, 86
Cascadia 81, 82
Central Coast Brewing 151
Coeur D'Alene Brewing/T. W. Fischer's Brewpub 183
Coopersmith's Pub and Brewery 177
Crazy Ed's Black Mountain Brewing 144
Crown City Brewing 152

D

Dead Cat Alley Brewery 66
Deschutes Brewery 128, 129
Durango Brewing 178

E

Eddie McStiff's Brewery 189
Electric Dave Brewery 145
Embudo Station/Sangre de Cristo Brewing 163
Etna Brewery 66, 67
Eugene City Brewing 129

F

Firestone and Fletcher Brewing 153
Fogg n' Suds 90, 91
Fort Spokane Brewery 109
Fullerton Hofbrau 154

G

Golden Pacific Brewery 45
Gordon-Biersch Brewery 45, 46
Gorkey's Cafe and Brewery 155
Granville Island Brewing 17, 83, 94, 95
Great American Beer Festival 21, 171

Great Northern Brewing 186

H

Hale's Ales 3, 110, 111, 112
Hart Brewing 113
Heritage Brewing 156
Hogshead Brewery 68
Honolulu Brewing 199
Hood River Brewery 129, 130
Hops Brewpub 141, 146
Horseshoe Bay Brewery 17, 88, 95
Hubcap Brewery 178
Humboldt Brewery 68
Huttenhain's Benecia Brewing 47

I

Institute of Brewing Studies 2, 15
Island Pacific/Vancouver Island
    Brewing 96

J

J & L Brewing 47

K

Kelmer's Brewhouse 56
KQED TV 39

L

Leeward Neighborhood Pub 97
Lind Brewing 47
Los Angeles Brewing/Eureka
    Brewery 157
Lost Coast Brewery 69

M

Mad River Brewery 70
Main Street Brewery 71
Mammoth Lakes Brewing 158
Marin Brewing 48
Maritime Pacific Brewing 114
McMenamin's Brewpubs 124,
    130-132
Mendocino Brewing 18, 38, 71, 72
Mission Brewing 158
Montana Brewing (Kessler) 170,
    187, 188
Monterey Brewing 57

N

Napa Valley Brewing/Calistoga
    Inn 57, 58
Nevada City Brewing 74
New Albion Brewery 15, 16, 20,
    33
New Brewer 1, 6
Noggins Westlake Brewpub 115
North Coast Brewery 73
Northwest Beer Journal 29, 86

O

Obispo Brewing 159
Odell Brewing 179
Okanagan Brewery 97, 98
Okie Girl Brewing 159
(Karl Strauss') Old Columbia
    Brewery 160
Old Colorado Brewing 179
Oregon Brewers Festival 23, 126
Oregon Trail Brewery 133, 134
Otto Brothers' Brewing 192

P

Pacific Brewing 200
Pacific Coast Brewing 48
Pacific Northwest Brewing 116
Pete's Brewing 49, 50
Pike Place Brewery 83, 85, 117
Pizza Deli and Brewery 134
Portland Brewing 135
Prairie Inn Cottage Brewery 98

R

Redhook Brewery 3, 83, 84, 118,
    119
Roger's Zoo 136
Rogue Brewery 136, 137
Roslyn Brewing 119, 120
Rubicon Brewing 75

S

San Andreas Brewing 58
San Francisco Brewing 50, 51
Salt Lake Brewing/Squatter's
    Brewpub 189
Santa Cruz Brewing 59

Santa Fe Brewing 164
Schirf Brewing/Wasatch Brewpub
    190, 191
Seabright Brewery 60
Seattle Brewing/Duwamps Cafe
    120
Shaftebury Brewery 98, 99
Shield's Brewing 161
Sierra Nevada Brewery 3, 16, 37,
    67, 76, 77
SLO Brewing 161
Snake River Brewing 184
Spinnakers Brewpub 100, 101
Stanislaus Brewery 61, 62
Star Spangled Beer 3, 5, 7
Strathcona Brewing 174
Sudwerk Privatbrauerei Hubsch
    77, 78
Sunshine Coast Brewery 101
Sun Valley Brewing 184

T

Telluride Brewing 180
Thomas Kemper Brewing 121
Tied House Cafe & Brewery 51
Triple Rock Brewery 52

Truckee Brewery 78, 79
Twenty Tank Brewery 53

U

Union Brewery 165, 166

W

Walnut Brewing 181
Whistler Brewing 101, 102
Willett's Brewing 63
Widmer Brewery 137, 138
Winchester Brewing 54
World Beer Review 1, 6
Wynkoop Brewery 181, 182

Y

Yakima Brewing & Malting 3, 17,
    122, 123
Yukon Brewing 198

Yes, I would like to order books from RedBrick Press

Brewery Adventures in the Wild West	0-941397-04-1	$14.95	_____
Star Spangled Beer: A Guide to America's New			
Microbreweries and Brewpubs	0-941397-00-9	$13.95	_____
Great Cooking With Beer	0-941397-02-5 (Hdbk)	$16.95	
	0-9413970-1-7 (Pb)	$10.95	_____
	Tax (VA 4 1/2%)		_____
	Shipping ($1.50/book)		_____
	TOTAL		_____

Please send information on RedBrick's books on specialty beers and
    microbreweries ☐

NAME_____

ADDRESS _____

CITY _____ STATE/PROVINCE _____ ZIP_____

Please send check or money order to:
RedBrick Press
P.O. Box 2184
Reston, VA 22090